Praise for *Buy the Avocado Toast*

Love it. A real book by a real person addressing a real problem in real life. Useful insights on how to have a different perspective on one's real (and perceived) problems.

—Clint Spurgeon, former CFO of Apple Japan

Stephanie's book lies at the heart of a central problem in America—and it's not just financial. Millenials are mired in student debt and can't find well-paid jobs that allow them to pay rent and interest on the loans. This has bred mental health problems and an opioid epidemic among those stuck at home who are 21–29. It suppresses the housing market and taxes our mental health system. Something needs to be done. Steph's book is a great start.

—Paul Schulte, founder of Schulte Research and author of *AI & Quantum Computing in Finance & Insurance*

Part financial self-help, part personal development, this book takes a radical look at the student debt crisis and offers fresh, out-of-the-box ideas on how to conquer six-figure student loan debt.

—Caroline Allen, author of the award-winning Elemental Journey series: *Earth*, *Air*, and *Fire*

This book provides a pathway and great practical approach for many people faced with painful student debt. A true testimonial from someone who has personally lived through this experience.

—Dana Robertson, senior director of pharmaceutical operations (retired), Medtronic

D0368061

Published by Familius LLC, www.familius.com
Familius books are available at special discounts for bulk purchases, whether for sales
promotions or for family or corporate use. For more information, contact Familius Sales
at 559-876-2170 or email orders@familius.com.

Library of Congress Control Number: 2019953185

Print ISBN 9781641702386
Ebook ISBN 9781641702843

Printed in the United States of America

Edited by Katharine Hale, Sarah Echard, and Peg Sandkam
Cover design by Carlos Guerrero
Book design by Brooke Jorden

10 9 8 7 6 5 4 3 2 1

First Edition

BUY THE AVOCADO TOAST

Dedicated to anyone who has dragged a suitcase of their belongings from secondhand store to secondhand store only to be told those possessions are worth literally nothing.

BUY THE AVOCADO TOAST

HOW TO
CRUSH STUDENT DEBT,
MAKE MORE MONEY,
AND LIVE YOUR BEST LIFE

Stephanie Bousley

CONTENTS

TWO PEOPLE WITH $100K+ STUDENT LOANS

Meet Ava.

Ava lives in New York City and is in her late twenties. She recently completed a master's degree in film—a creative field she loves—at a top university. She started applying for jobs three months *before* graduation but only managed to land an unpaid internship. Her boss is younger than her and never went to grad school. She is hoping to make connections that will lead to paid work soon. She would be happy to find something that pays a $40,000–$50,000 salary and offers health insurance—although even that is not a very livable salary in New York.

She rents a room in a tiny apartment for $1,000 per month with a guy she met on Craigslist. Her roommate rarely showers and appears to spend most days playing video games, but that doesn't seem to affect his ability to pay bills on time. Working weekends as a nanny for a Wall Street family pays Ava's bills. Sixty-hour workweeks don't leave much time to work on her passion: screenwriting.

Ava took out $216,000 in student loans to pay for graduate school. She exercised the deferred payment option while attending, as her job as a teaching assistant only covered basic living expenses. The loans have been accumulating interest at a rate of 8.5% since she took them out, and the interest compounds every year. Upon graduation, she consolidated her loans and applied for income-based repayment through the US government, which required her to pay back only $386 a month. These payments don't even cover the interest the debt accumulates each month, so although she never misses a payment, her debt continues to grow. The last time she checked the balance, it was $286,000.

Ava feels like a failure. Thinking about her situation during long subway rides often makes her cry. It is baffling how she, the person voted "Most Likely to Succeed" in high school and who graduated *magna cum laude* with a double major from a university that she attended on a full-ride academic scholarship, would wind up owing almost $300,000 to anyone. Based on existing evidence, she will never pay it off. She figures she should go ahead and forget about ever owning a house, having a wedding, or even getting married—the successful, ambitious, and educated people she's interested in dating avoid girls in her financial situation. Spending money on *anything*, even tampons, causes inordinate amounts of guilt. She has no emergency fund nor retirement plan. Drinking is the only thing that provides temporary relief from the daily onslaught of shame and anxiety. All she can really do is hope that within the next twenty years, US legislation changes the income-based repayment plan to *not* treat student debt forgiveness as taxable income because otherwise, twenty years from now she'll owe almost $250,000 in taxes for her "forgiven" student loans and have to apply for bankruptcy.

Now meet Ava's classmate, Sarah.

Sarah works twelve hours a day at a five-billion-dollar hedge fund as personal assistant to the CEO. She makes $160,000 a year and lives in Singapore with her boyfriend, another expatriate whose work package comes with a fully paid apartment and car. For weekend get-aways, they visit Bangkok, Bali, and the Maldives. Winters find them skiing in Japan. Sarah has not done her own laundry or washed dishes in years, as she can easily employ a housecleaner to come once a week for about $120 a month. She used her first year's bonus to buy a small condo in the United States, and the mortgage is fully paid each month by the tenant who lives there.

Sarah also has high student loan debt—five figures (down from six)—but she is able to comfortably pay a few thousand toward the balance each month without major sacrifices to her lifestyle. Next year's bonus (at least $70,000, if this year is any indication) will almost clear the remainder. Her student loans have long since been refinanced to 3.4 percent interest, so her payments always take a nice bite out of the principal.

Sarah pays a writing coach to help her continue to work toward her goal of being a screenwriter. After winning a few screenwriting contests and getting a manager in Los Angeles, she remains optimistic enough to continue. She pays off the balance of her credit card in full every month and has accumulated enough points to fly both of her parents out for a free visit.

Sarah has been sober five years. Her emergency fund has $25,000, most of which is robo-invested online for an average return of about 6 percent, and her retirement fund is growing too. Life isn't perfect, but there are many things to be grateful for.

Full disclosure: There is no Ava, nor Sarah. They're both me—at different points in my life. I've had to get far enough away from being one and comfortable enough being the other to even begin to tell this story, because my six-figure student loan debt was a cloak of shame I wore silently for years. I was so overwhelmed with what I owed that I could barely function.

Let me be clear—I never set out to author personal finance books or become some debt expert. I have a different full-time job. I am just a person who had a particular set of experiences that I wanted to share in order to help other people with student loan debt or fears that they have failed in life because of their financial situations. I got up at

4:45 a.m. for a year and a half to write this book because none of the other financial self-help books I read seemed to offer solutions for people who *aren't* chronic overspenders, who were generally thought of as overachievers in life, and who can't micromanage their budgets into a payment plan that will get them out of debt as fast as they'd like. I've written this book to give people hope that they, like me, can transition from a life of suffering and shame to one of comfort and hope.

When I turned to other financial self-help books, I often felt they were condescending and implied I, the reader, was in debt primarily because I had spent money recklessly, charging up things I couldn't afford on credit cards. They also all involved doing budgets. Supposedly, the answer to my debt problem was in endless amounts of expense tracking and a hyperawareness of every incoming and outgoing cent. For a while, I believed it, and I proceeded to download countless iPhone apps, freaking out if I forgot to log my salad at work or a taxi fare. I second-guessed everything that involved spending money: *Did I really need soy milk in my cappuccino? Heat? Dry cleaning? Breakfast?* I adopted the motto, "If you must buy something, you must buy the cheapest version humanly possible." I sold every possession I didn't need on eBay or Craigslist. I stopped eating healthy food, having a gym membership, and seeing movies in the theater. I was miserable.

The debt books promised my misery would last only a short time—until my debt was paid off. Only a few more years, right? Not really. At the rate I was going, with the $1,600 of interest that accumulated every month, I would be living this way for about thirteen more years. The thought of doing that made me want to kill myself. I don't mean that in the melodramatic sense. I actually thought things were so bad—with no end in sight—that there was no point in living anymore. I had worked hard all my life, and for what? There was nothing to show for it. I actually felt as though *all* of my dreams were out of reach, I would never be able to do what I loved, and I would be a prisoner to working jobs I completely hated forever, mainly because of this debt.

As of this publication, there are no formal studies that I'm aware of specifically aimed at a link between suicide and high student loan debt, but the internet is replete with blogs, articles, and comments speaking to the growing hopelessness of indebted individuals.[1] We do know that dentists, doctors, and veterinarians have historically higher suicide rates compared to other professions,[2] and we also know that graduates tend to leave those degree programs with high amounts of student loan debt. In short, it's an issue people are starting to pay more attention to.

Growing up in the '80s, I thought that having a successful career was a formula, easy to figure out and execute: get into a good school, work hard, go to more school if you have to, learn as much as you can, get a good job, and stay at that job until you get promoted a few times. My observations told me that people who did this were usually married (and had thrown lovely weddings), owned a house, had some kids, and, depending on their career field, enjoyed varied degrees of comfort.

I finished undergrad with less than $10,000 of debt, which I quickly paid off. My undergraduate program cost $36,000 per year, but I took advantage of the tools available and came out on top: academic scholarships, three jobs, and a Resident Advisor position that provided free dorm housing and a meal plan. It was tough, but when I finished, numerous employment opportunities were being thrown my way. It seemed it had all been worthwhile. I took a job at an art gallery, worked there for a few years, and then decided I wanted to go back to school.

Here's where things started going wrong. I used the same logic that many students use when trying to figure out their careers. I wanted to go to school for filmmaking. I knew filmmaking was a risky industry, so I thought, *If I am going to try to make a go of this, I must get the best education possible.* I applied only to the best programs, which I thought would lead me to the most promising jobs. If I didn't get in to any of the top schools, I wouldn't go at all. Fortunately (or unfortunately, depending on how you look at it), I got into New York University's Tisch School of the Arts—the Harvard of film schools, with only thirty-six people accepted per year out of hundreds, an acceptance rate of 9 percent. When I got the call, I was on my way to work. I started crying and jumping up and down on the street outside of my office.

About five years later, I was crying again, but for a different reason: soul-crushing debt. There were no job prospects knocking at my door. It was 2010, in the middle of the financial crisis, and there were no jobs to be had anywhere. The system was no longer on my side. I couldn't find the tools. In fact, there didn't seem to be any means—only a resounding mantra from the few people I wasn't too humiliated to talk to about my debt: *Maybe you shouldn't have gone to grad school.* Not very helpful.

How did I go from six-figure student loans to an international career in finance? Here's what happened. My university had a study abroad program that gave me a "student pass," a visa that would allow me to work and take classes in Singapore. Knowing nothing about Singapore other than it could provide a change of scenery from the depressing state of affairs back home, I took the plunge and signed up.

In Singapore, where I expected to stay only a short time, I put up an ad on Craigslist: "Ex-Hollywood Personal Assistant for Hire," stating that I was a mature and responsible American looking for part-time work while I finished my studies. I had never actually worked as a personal assistant, but I had interned in production companies in both Hollywood and New York City. Within a week, an American woman contacted me. She had also just moved to Singapore from New York City with her husband and young children and needed some help with getting organized and babysitting. I started working for her a few hours a week at the equivalent of $14.50 per hour.

My incredibly small income would not be enough to survive in Singapore, a place where rent is 31 percent higher than in the United States.[3] I quickly learned, to my extreme disappointment, that having my own *bedroom* was now a luxury I couldn't afford, so I rented a shared room in an apartment in the red-light district (a part of Singapore known as "Geylang") and lived with a group of French exchange students. I shared a bedroom with one of the students, Chanel, who was twenty-one (I was almost thirty). We slept on two separate twin beds in the same room, just like I did when I was eighteen years old and living in my college dorm. We each had one wardrobe. It was not a happy time. Dating was pretty much out of the question, as I could not bear the thought of explaining my living situation to anyone. I had no privacy to write screenplays or do my creative work.

Besides the living environment, every day was full of small, private humiliations, thumping home the conviction that I had made serious wrong turns in my life. A particularly bad day found me on the side of the road, cleaning up a screaming five-year-old who had just vomited banana milkshake all over herself and the car. A slightly better one involved running a toddler through a luxury rug store as he peed over every single carpet. It just didn't seem right that hours of sitting in filmmaking practicums with Oscar-winning directors would result in me standing knee-high in a McDonald's ball pit at 3:00 p.m. every Tuesday or chasing children through plastic tunnels at Go-Go Bambini. I felt like a complete fool, going into six-figure student loan debt for *this*. Something had gone terribly wrong, and it felt terminal, cataclysmic, and cruel.

So there I was in Singapore, finishing my thesis film projects and working as a babysitter, thinking I would definitely move back to the States when I had finished school. Hopefully the economy would improve. Maybe one day I would be able to walk to my neighborhood subway stop without carrying a keychain of pepper spray, en route to picking up my boss's kids from a private preschool almost as expensive as NYU. During this time, I filled a lot of my free time with drinking—because I was depressed and unable to escape the constant feeling of failure. It is funny how the stereotype of "broke artist loser" can snowball into an authentic version of itself.

Even more depressing was the isolation I felt. Sure, there were other expats in Singapore—it wasn't like I was in rural China. But there were almost no artists, no creative people; if you saw a Caucasian person walking on the street, there was an 80 percent chance they worked in finance and a 20 percent chance they were a non-working spouse. Not one person I met was a film student working as a babysitter. That I was even doing *that* was amazing, because pretty much everyone in Singapore has a maid from the Philippines or Indonesia to watch their children.

I finished my degree and began looking for film jobs in Singapore. There were none—or so it seemed. When I inquired in person at production companies who had posted jobs online, they denied having any openings. After a few months of searching for full-time work, my student pass was about to expire. I told my boss I would be moving back to the United States soon. She was sad to hear it. By that time, I was doing a lot more than just babysitting for her; my duties had expanded to include housesitting, events, and personal assistant work while the children were at school. She said she would ask around and see if any of her friends wanted to hire me and get me a work pass through their companies.

Shortly thereafter, I received a job offer to be a personal assistant at her husband's hedge fund for about $73,000 per year, plus full benefits and a "discretionary" annual bonus (which later turned out to be $45,000). Add to this the fact that I'd be able to write off my US taxes under the foreign-earned income exclusion and pay a minimal Singapore income tax of 5 percent, and it was too good of an offer to turn down. It got me an employment pass, which allowed me to stay in Singapore for another year as long as I only worked for this asset management company. They didn't even mind my very visible tattoos.

I fell into a situation that would end up being my saving grace, but it didn't feel like that in the beginning. My first year at the hedge fund proved to be the most difficult of my life. Before the job, I thought things couldn't get much worse, but I was wrong. I had to report to the office at 6:45 a.m. and sometimes worked as late as midnight. It was an uncreative environment driven by money and testosterone. Working on the trade floor with my boss, I was screamed at daily for not understanding the business better. For months, I completely stopped writing screenplays and, for the most part, watching movies. The stress kept me up at night, and for a while, I was prescribed antidepressants and sleeping pills just to function.

But one thing was happening: I was paying down my student loans more rapidly than I ever thought possible. Over the next three years, I adjusted to the work, got better at the job, and made more money. Before I knew it, I had paid off the first hundred thousand dollars.

Eventually, I even figured out how to write and continue making films in spite of my schedule. Best of all, I learned a lot about money from my new environment.

I look back now at the path that got me here, the path that I want to share with you. Here are the takeaways: First, I began by legally getting into an economically sound foreign country. Second, as soon as I got there, I hooked up with other Americans. Next, I took people up on job offers, even if it was outside my career. While I happened to connect with the first American woman through Craigslist, I also could have joined the American Association, the American Women's Association, the American Club, or any number of expatriate social groups where Americans might have gone. I firmly believe that regardless of what country you are from and what country you're in, there are people you can meet who will help you. In a foreign country, people join forces in ways that just don't happen at home. If I were still in New York City studying film, I probably wouldn't have come to meet one of the most successful hedge fund managers on Wall Street. In Singapore, we were just two people in Asia trying to find a decent bagel.

I do not cry on the subway anymore. I do not think I have failed at life. I took a big risk by going to graduate school (which I neglected to see as a risk in the first place) that didn't pan out as I thought it would. The consequences were enormous, and thus equally significant actions were required to recover from them. I had to think way, way outside of the box to even get close to conquering my debt. I can now see the light at the end of the tunnel and expect to be fully debt-free in only a few more years.

People reading this might worry: *Do I have to work at a job I don't like for years before doing what I love?* No! While working, I produced a music video of a Swedish musician for Sony. I produced two short films for former classmates and friends. I wrote two award-winning TV pilot screenplays that attracted a manager from Los Angeles, and I've even explored photography and exhibited some of my photos.

There are alternatives to forcing yourself to live on practically nothing while you perpetually punish yourself for your financial situation. This is not a book about working abroad or doing the exact same things I did. It *is* about paying off high student debt using the skills and options most readily available—in essence, to create *your version* of the debt payoff success story by putting a few ideas in your head that might not have been there before. I'm not going to encourage you to duplicate the path I followed to get out of debt; nobody's success can be re-created exactly. Instead, you're going to get a book of somewhat controversial ideas that can, if applied correctly, provide a huge leg up on your current payoff strategy. Some are easier to execute than others. However, pretty much anyone with any educational background in any amount of debt can make some of them work. So if you're ready to think about unconventional ways to improve your finances and life, read on!

Notes

1. Johannsen, C. C. (2012, July 2). The ones we've lost: The student loan debt suicides. *Huffington Post*. Retrieved September 18, 2018, from https://www.huffingtonpost.com/c-cryn-johannsen/student-loan-debt-suicides_b_1638972.html.

2. Hornsby, T. (Updated 2018, October 12). How student loans kill people by contributing to suicide and how to break the cycle. Student Loan Planner. Retrieved September 18, 2018, from https://www.studentloanplanner.com/student-loan-debt-suicide/.

3. Cost of living in Singapore. (2017, August 1). Numbeo. Retrieved August 23, 2017, from http://www.numbeo.com/cost-of-living/country_result.jsp?country=Singapore.

CHAPTER 1

COPY HOW THE RICH THINK ABOUT THEMSELVES

I've always compared budgeting to being on a diet. To lose weight, it seems like a good idea to restrict calories, write down everything you eat, have a weekly plan of what to eat, and so forth. However, being too restrictive often results in a binge-eating relapse. My experience is that money is similar. If I punish myself for spending money or if I stop allowing comforts of any kind, I'm likely to fall off the wagon and eventually spend money in a way that makes me feel like crap.

What bothered me about other debt books is that they seemed so restrictive and patronizing, like the answer to my financial situation was in punishing myself for the rest of my life. It was like I was a child being told everything would be OK if I just gave up Starbucks and HBO. While the author may have been at one time in debt, usually it was from reckless spending in combination with forces outside of their control, not from student loan debt and predatory lending. How could that person relate to me and what I was going through?

I guess I'm a person who doesn't like to be told what to do. For some reason, the idea of a person labeling himself or herself an "expert" on debt and personal finance seems intrinsically irritating to me. I always felt that people who make a living speaking about financial self-help have little to offer me because, unlike them, I am not trying to reinvent myself as an expert about money or get a million Instagram followers. I simply want to deal with my financial problems and get back to the life I was trying to lead before the debt—as quickly as possible.

Furthermore, their advice always seemed to focus on lower levels of debt and on low-hanging fruit. Many "Get Out of Debt" seminars broadly advertise that one can get out of debt *on any income!* Do they think people in debt can't do math? How was I going to pay off $286,000 of debt while living in a major metropolitan city, paying rent, and working for entry-level money at an organization where people much more senior than I were barely making ends meet? In that scenario, it did not seem like a debt-free life would be coming anytime soon.

This is the difference between books that address $30,000 debt versus those that deal with $300,000 debt: What if instead of a restrictive diet, people in even excessive debt were encouraged to live comfortably, take vacations, pursue interests, and hire cleaners, trainers, and coaches? Most outsiders would think people with six-figure debt wanting holidays and a cleaner are incredibly stupid, arrogant, or both. Are they?

After I started working in finance and got used to being surrounded by millionaires every day, I noticed they were singing a different tune—one that resonated with me more than the existing debt books. Instead of focusing on what wasn't there (lack of money), they focused on what *was* there (money). At the time, money seemed extremely abstract and out of reach. But somehow, as if by osmosis, the longer I stayed in that environment, the more money eventually flowed into my bank account.

I hear what you're saying: "I am an artist/journalist/public defense attorney/human rights lawyer/[insert whatever profession that resulted in six-figure student loan debt here]. Money was never important to me. I'm not trying to become some sociopath on Wall Street."

I get it. I thought the same thing. I used to detest rich people too—until I realized understanding them could help me get out of debt faster. The black-and-white thinking was getting me nowhere—there are jerks working at nonprofits and friendly people working at banks. Plus, if developing even a one percent "Wall Street" part of your brain can help you get off the path of debt and back on the road of your dreams, isn't some experimentation worth it?

Here's a few things I learned from observing people with more money than me. I learned the following life lessons by *observation only*. Rich people would never actually say these things, but when you are surrounded by them, it seems they all feel this way.

Lesson #1: You are special.

Trust me: *all* rich people seem to think this about themselves. The belief floods every fiber of their being. It informs the way they dress, live, and spend their money. "Normal" clothes, shoes, cars, and houses just aren't good enough! Who really needs a five-thousand-dollar handbag? A special person.

Of course, they don't want you to know they are thinking this. Society demands they are humble, grateful, and kind at all times, saying things like, "I guess I just got lucky." They love recounting some earlier period of life where they were operating a business from a garage, surviving only on cans of baked beans. They tip well, look people in the eye when shaking hands, and never miss a "please" or "thank you."

But take it from a person who has worked for individuals and families worth eight to ten figures: every single one of these people on some level really and truly thinks that if a person in the family forgot his passport, laws should be forgone and the whole family should still be able to land in any foreign airport since they are on a private jet. And most of the time, in spite of the missing passport, they can.

How does this type of thinking apply to a person in six-figure debt? When I first started working as a nanny, I had to catch a bus forty-five minutes before my shift and then walk twenty minutes in ninety-degree heat to my employers' gated community. I did this for over a year before I discovered the cleaner took taxis to and from work every day and requested reimbursement from our employers. I never even thought to ask for that. In my way of thinking, one got oneself to work each day on one's own dime. Like the cleaner, I began taking taxis after this, which my employers paid for.

I have spent most of my life thinking about why I don't deserve things I want or need from existing or potential employers:

- I wouldn't want to upset them.
- I wouldn't want someone to think I'm weird, entitled, or spoiled.
- I should just be grateful for what I have.
- Life is not fair.
- Nobody else asks for that.
- People do not progress in that way.
- Other people don't get paid that much for this work.

Rich people don't think this way. Even if no one else is getting what they're asking for, they fully believe they should. Why? Because they are special.

How can you start thinking you are deserving of special treatment, particularly if you've had decades of experience not thinking that way? By acting *as if*. Ever hear the phrase "Bring the body, and the mind will follow"? You don't have to feel different and extraordinary at first, as long as you start *taking the actions* of someone who does. Start asking for additional comforts in small situations and rejecting discomfort. Here are some (somewhat silly) suggestions:

- Go to an expensive store or boutique. Have a salesperson help you learn about a product or try on clothing, and if you don't find something you love, just thank them nicely for the help and leave without buying anything. Don't make excuses for why you are not making a purchase.

- Hire someone to do a small job for you, like organize your computer files, cook and freeze some meals, or mow the lawn. Tell them, unapologetically, what needs to be done. Refuse to feel guilty about it. If they do something wrong, kindly point it out and ask them to redo it.
- Send a meal back at a restaurant if you don't like it or it was not prepared to your specifications.
- The next time you are negotiating or buying anything—a work contract, a lease, a car, a purchase off Craigslist—ask for something additional to the initial offer: a travel allowance, other discounts, insurance reimbursements. Wait twenty-four hours for a response.
- Ask your landlord to make some small and not entirely necessary improvement to your living quarters, such as painting a wall or replacing an appliance that doesn't quite work. It does not matter whether the thing happens. What matters is that you asked.

None of these things cost much money, and to someone not used to acting this way, they may seem outright ridiculous and rude. If you think they seem harsh, ask yourself why. Is it because you are habitually more concerned with other people's feelings and financial situations than your own?

What is the connection between these behaviors and getting out of debt? Think of it this way: Does an individual with this mindset get lowballed on jobs or stuck paying the tip on the company lunch bill? No. Do they end up paying to get their dry cleaning done twice when the first place failed to whiten the whites enough? No. Bring the body, and the mind will follow.

Warren Buffet is famous for saying, "I always knew I'd be rich. I never doubted it for a second."[1] He didn't seem to dwell on the fact his undergrad degree was from the University of Nebraska–Lincoln, and not an Ivy League school. It did not stop him from amassing 84 billion dollars (as of spring 2018).[2] I couldn't care less about Warren

Buffett, and I certainly don't believe that you can just *think* your way out of excessive student loan debt. The point is simply that rich people think they are different and special—and you should too. This ties in perfectly to the next lesson:

Lesson #2: Sometimes the rules don't apply to you.

In Journal #4, Henry David Thoreau wrote, "Any fool can make a rule. And any fool will mind it." When I worked with millionaires, I often overheard my coworkers on the phone during lunch breaks on the phone, having a certain kind of call. The calls focused on one topic: getting out of paying for something. It could be anything—a parking ticket, a credit card penalty, import tax, library fees, cell phone bills, bank charges. The more standard the charge, the more convinced they are that they should be exempt. Whether or not they actually spoke on the phone for three hours while roaming seems irrelevant. They don't feel they should have to pay, and they are prepared to argue with the person on the phone until they get their way. More often than not, they do.

Before I went to graduate school, I worked as a technical recruiter in Silicon Valley. This was in the early 2000s, and business was booming. When we were trying to sell a potential employee to a client on the phone, our company was annoyingly strict about sticking to the lines we were given to say. Whenever we encountered a client repeatedly telling us no, we had to put the call on hold to get guidance from our team leader.

My boss, John,[3] was a twenty-four-year-old Cornell alumnus probably making around $225,000 a year. I had just sent a candidate named Arjun in for an interview with a manager who had found issues with the seven candidates I'd sent him previously. Our fee was thirty percent of the placed candidate's first-year salary, which in this case was $150,000. The manager's thought process and pickiness were understandable to me. If he was going to pay a recruitment agency $45,000 to find someone, he wanted to make sure the person was worth it. As

I listened on the phone to the manager's concerns about Arjun, they made sense. He didn't feel Arjun would mesh with the team, and he wanted a candidate with more experience in certain technologies.

I listened patiently and took notes on all his concerns. "I'll target those things for the next candidate I show you," I told him.

John motioned for me to put the call on hold. "What's going on?"

"He didn't like Arjun," I explained.

"Arjun is awesome; why not?"

I listed the issues the manager had. John cut me off.

"You're going to pick up the phone and tell the manager to just hire Arjun," he said emphatically.

"But he just said Arjun's not right for the job," I stammered. This went against everything I thought about human relationships. I wanted this manager to trust me, and I wanted to give him exactly what he wanted. I believed $45,000 was a *lot* of money.

"We've already sent him several candidates, and he's had problems with every single one. He's not going to find a unicorn, and at this rate, he'll never find someone he likes. Rather than wait for the perfect candidate who will never come, it's your job to convince him to hire Arjun. So pick up the phone and tell him," John instructed.

Arjun started the job about a month later. He was still in the job a year later when I lost contact. John believed the usual rules of engagement between a client and a recruiter just didn't apply to him. When he was right, it paid off.

So I'm supposed to go around making ridiculous demands for things I'm not entitled to? The answer is yes and no. There are times when acting this way just makes you look like a jerk. Other times, when what you have to lose is significantly less than what you have to gain, there is no reason not to do it.

When I was trying to refinance my student loans, I had no cosigner (nobody wanted to put their name on my $286,000 debt—I don't blame them). My only chance of getting the refinancing was to prove I was making good money and had perfect credit. The only problem was that my credit wasn't perfect and wouldn't be for another year and a half. I had a delinquency after moving apartments several years ago (I never received the bill), and it was stuck on my credit record for seven years.

I called the credit card company and asked them to remove it, which they were unwilling to do. Begrudgingly, I coughed up $1,600 every month in interest fees as my student loan interest rate remained at 8.5 percent. My anger and resentment toward the lending company, my university, and myself were at an all-time high.

During this time, something prompted me to seek legal advice to find out if there was any other way to get the rate lowered. The lawyer taught me a technique to deal with the credit card and rating bureaus, and in less than two months, my credit was back up to excellent. (See Chapter 6 for full details.) A month later, I had refinanced my student loans to a rate of 2.34 percent, and my monthly interest payments were a little over $400. By thinking the rules did not apply to me, I was able to pay the same amount toward my loans each month but with an extra $1,200 going toward the principal balance.

Lesson #3: Money opens doors.

Comedian Chris Rock once said, "Wealth is not about having a lot of money. It's about having a lot of options."[4] Money gives people the opportunity to expand their horizons and live life to the fullest, whereas being financially deficient narrows our life view. Money creates choices.

The three most visible areas where money opens doors are health, security, and education. The connection between money and better health care is well documented.[5] My Aunt Carol died after a seven-year battle with amyloidosis, a disease causing buildup of abnormal protein in the organs. The treatment is similar to that for cancer: chemotherapy and pills. She did chemotherapy several times and was pronounced disease-free three years after diagnosis. Unfortunately, the condition returned, eventually claiming her life after four more long years of suffering, which included kidney removal and dialysis.

Contrast this scenario with former Tour de France cyclist Lance Armstrong. Initially diagnosed with stage 3 cancer, his physician Dr. Reeves later said that his chance of survival was "almost zero."[6]

Armstrong had already acquired some wealth, having won the USPRO Championship in Philadelphia, placed in the Tour de France, and celebrated a solo win at the 1993 World Pro Race Championship in Norway. No doubt Armstrong's winning attitude contributed to his survival, but his money almost certainly gave him access to more treatment options than my Aunt Carol. With money comes better health insurance, access to alternative and preventative treatments not covered by insurance, and additional support like dieticians, gym memberships, and personal training.

Money also creates options in terms of security. In his book *Solving the Wealth Puzzle*, Anthony Deemer says:

> One good definition of security is *freedom from anxiety or fear*. To have a real sense of safety and security, regardless of how much money we have or do not have, we need:
> - enough good food to eat;
> - shelter for us and our families;
> - good health, which also means good health care;
> - safety and a sense of security;
> - security for our old age, including health care and living conditions;
> - people who love and support us;
> - the ability to help others;
> - the desire to positively affect the world we live in;
> - to leave a legacy for our family and/or our community; and
> - to have enough possessions to make life easier.[7]

Finally, there's education. If you went to a top school and you're not rich, you probably found yourself surrounded by rich kids much of the time. Maybe you wondered whether they actually deserved to be there or if their parents had made a large donation to the school.

Here's an interesting fact: On April 17, 2015, researchers at the Massachusetts Institute of Technology (MIT) and Harvard University reported that the academic "achievement gap" between lower-income and higher-income children is actually reflected in brain anatomy.[8] For the study, researchers compared MRI brain imaging scans of high- and low-income students. They found that the higher-income students had thicker brain cortexes in both the temporal and occipital lobes—areas associated with visual perception and knowledge accumulation. The differences in cortical thickness correlated directly with differences in both test scores and family income. These differences in brain structure were also associated with one measure of academic achievement: the students from higher-income families had higher scores on standardized tests.[9]

How do ordinary people from a background of average financial means compete in a society where the most well-to-do literally have better brains? For starters, we can become more sophisticated at identifying opportunities to make up ground.

When I was a teaching assistant at NYU, I got asked to speak at a class called Exit Strategies, which was supposed to help film students in their final semester of school prepare to graduate and enter the workforce. My question to the students was: "Let's say you move to Los Angeles after graduate school with the goal of directing a movie as soon as possible. You are offered two potential jobs: one as a production assistant on a movie, paying the industry standard of $125 a day, or another as a household manager for an elderly rich man, paying $25 an hour. Which will be better for your career?"

They were less than excited to hear that my suggestion was the elderly man. Some even became angry. The path to Hollywood greatness is one we had been hearing about for years: get your foot in the door through any means possible, pass your script to someone in the industry, then he'll introduce you to the right people, you'll make a good impression, and BAM, you're in!

I interned in both LA and New York during graduate school and met no one who had made that leap. We all heard the story one too many times of Quentin Tarantino meeting producer Lawrence Bender while working at a video rental store and being rocketed to success. My experience was entirely different. After serving various unpaid internships in both New York and Los Angeles, no one wanted to read my scripts. When I asked my production manager boss on a film I was working on (for free) whether he saw me getting paid employment as a result of this internship with the company, he told me that he worked in a bakery on the weekends just to make ends meet. Then he flat-out said, "No."

Let's say I had taken the job with the wealthy elderly man in Hollywood at $25 an hour. First, if someone is living in a mansion in Beverly Hills, it's highly likely that he either knows people in the industry or used to work in it himself. Second, if he's not working anymore, he probably has lots of free time for you, so the two of you can build a relationship. And third (and I admit this is a bit of a stretch), the fact that he's nearing the end of his life might mean he's looking to do something meaningful for some young, sharp person.

Of course, spending $100,000 to $300,000 on a degree and then working at a job that requires no degree feels depressing. But the reality is, working as a practically unpaid production assistant (and perhaps having a second job) for twelve to sixteen hours a day leaves very little time for making creative work. On the other hand, working eight hours for an elderly person leaves an extra four to eight hours in your day for attending Hollywood networking events, writing, planning your next shoot, and so forth.

The reason most wealthy people work isn't because they love working or they love making money. They work now to later maintain their standard of living in retirement, and given how long they're likely to live, this requires a vast reservoir of money. In other words, they're working for high pay to free up time later. No rich person sees sense in a work equation where you have no time to do what you want and no way to stockpile money for the future.

Lesson #4: Put yourself first.

I remember we once hired someone at my hedge fund who, when asked about salary expectations, said he was expecting a *minimum* $2 million base with a guaranteed $2 million bonus for the first two years.

Before working in finance, I was in the dreadful habit of giving potential employers a break. With new jobs, I never handled the salary negotiation part well. It's almost as if I thought everyone was as broke as I was.

In my first job after college, I worked at a small art gallery/nightlife space in San Francisco. It was inconveniently located in the Sunset District, which was mostly known as a local watering hole. I accepted full-time work at a starting salary of $28,000. Over the course of two years, I increased my salary to $40,000 and established the venue as a go-to spot for up-and-coming artists and musicians.

I applied for a music promotion job at a much larger nightclub downtown and got it. The owner asked me about my compensation requirements. The last place I worked had been struggling financially, and I did not want to offend my new boss by looking like I didn't understand how hard it was to make money as a nightlife space in the city.

"Well," I stammered, "I was making $40,000 at my last job. If I could at least hit that, I'd be happy." Guess what he paid me? $40,000. Now who makes a career move *in their existing field* to earn the same salary they made at their last job? Didn't my years of experience qualify me for a raise?

I was not putting myself first. I was putting my boss first—a boss who, just like my last boss, was an investment banker at Goldman Sachs who owned a nightclub for fun. I was more concerned about this guy's business surviving than surviving myself! Incidentally, when I resigned from that job less than a year later, the owner immediately offered me a raise to $52,000 a year, stating he had been prepared to pay that from the beginning.

Do you ever project your poverty onto other people and situations, thinking that because you are struggling, everyone is? Maybe you should stop doing that. Believe instead that there is money for the taking—and that if you don't take it, someone else will. It's not about thinking your debt will magically disappear; it's about not making your debt situation worse by underselling yourself. Rich people don't do it—neither should you.

Lesson #5: Having money isn't bad.

If you were to Google "quotes about wealth," the following phrases would appear:

- *Where wealth accumulates, men decay.* —Oliver Goldsmith
- *You aren't wealthy until you have something money can't buy.* —Anonymous
- *The real measure of your wealth is how much you'd be worth if you lost all your money.* —Bernard Meltzer
- *Much wealth brings many enemies.* —Swahili proverb
- *Wealth consists not in having great possessions but in having few wants.* —Epictetus

The list goes on. When I was in graduate film school, in the process of going into six-figure student loan debt, I was surrounded by kids from well-to-do families, who seemed to be better positioned for success in the art world. I saw them not only get their graduate degrees paid for by people who weren't them, but many also received over $100,000 to make their thesis or first feature film. They lived comfortably, and upon graduating, they moved into better apartments (in New York) or houses (in LA) where they focused on gaining work experience. I later learned this was not at all uncommon. The lesser-privileged students (like my friends and me) would create the following narratives about them:

- "She might have money, but she has nothing to say [creatively]."
- "He can't write a good script because he's been sheltered by money his whole life, and he knows it."
- "She might be getting work in New York, but it's just because her parents are paying for her entire life."
- "The only reason that film went to Sundance was because his family made a huge donation."
- "Don't work for him. He'll convince you to help for free even though he has more than enough money to pay."

I realized this was a narrative that wasn't helping me at all. Why? By convincing myself that everyone with money was untalented, unhappy, "just" lucky, and out to take advantage of others, I was forced to accept the reverse as well:

- I would never be able to live comfortably and focus on my creative career.
- I would not be able to make films nor take them to film festivals to help establish my name in the industry.
- Rich people get ahead by luck and manipulation of others; thus, because I have no luck and am not willing to use people, I will not get ahead.

In other words, if I never accepted that I was the cause of my money problem, I could never move past blaming others and become a part of the solution.

Before I worked in finance, I saw the world in very black-and-white terms: the haves and the have-nots. I was a have-not and subconsciously believed I would stay there. But—and I never would have said this aloud—I did things a lot of rich people don't do: continued going into extreme debt, worked for free, surrounded myself with other financially challenged folks, lived in a crappy apartment with crappy people, and constantly talked about what a bad situation I was in.

I *desperately* did not want to be a have-not. In fact, part of the reason I had chosen to attend one of the best graduate programs in my field was due to the hope that it would help me get out of that category. However, it actually started with convincing myself that *broke for life* wasn't written on my forehead for the whole world to see.

By the sheer experience of being surrounded by millionaires in a work setting, my narrative has slowly shifted:

- Many people are rich, and I can be too.
- Many people work in the industry they are in to have the freedom to eventually do something else while they're still relatively young, and I can as well.
- There is nothing wrong with reinvesting some of the money you make in yourself.
- Comfort makes me a happier, more generous, more relaxed person.
- If people already have money, good for them! Maybe I can learn something from them.

Wealthy people don't talk about the money they have because they are aware of the backlash that will follow. They are acutely aware that if they speak about how much better flying business class is than economy, how it feels to pay someone for performing quality work that helps you get ahead, and the sense of pride that comes with receiving a bonus equivalent to several additional years of pay (or more), everyone would hate them. So they keep quiet. Just remember: not talking about money doesn't mean that money is inherently *bad*. Money solves a lot of problems, and it's not a crime to want it.

Lesson #6: Wealth is a choice.

This probably sounds obvious. Who chooses to be poor? When I was drowning in six-figure student loan debt, I felt I had no options, and I resented rich people. During the beginning of my stint in finance, I dated a Harvard alum working in corporate law and capital markets. Once, he invited me to meet him and his friends at a bar called One Altitude in Singapore. It was an expensive rooftop bar where finance and corporate types hung out after work. At age thirty, I had never worked in a corporate job. I didn't even own corporate clothing. I felt so out of place accepting the invitation. I was also intimidated by his friends (and even by him). I declined and told him I had a birthday party to attend and went to a dive bar with my friend instead. During the night, I sent him this text: "You're with your people; I'm with mine."

Is it any surprise the relationship didn't work out? The point is not that I was at a dive bar; it is that I thought I couldn't go anywhere else. I had become so insecure by what I didn't have and the amount of debt I did have that it was impossible for me to feel comfortable around wealthy, successful people. I had put this guy on a massive pedestal. I thought if I could "get" him, I would be less of a loser. My future might be more secure. He represented a life that I wanted but thought I was unworthy of. This limiting belief dictated where I lived, ate, shopped, and parked; it even affected who I associated with. If I couldn't go to the same *bar* as successful corporate types, how was I going to work around them five days a week?

Being rich and being poor are both choices. You may not have chosen the circumstances that got you to either place, but you can opt to *take the actions* of a person who believes they will someday be successful instead of the actions of someone who won't. In the past, the implication that I struggled financially because I somehow chose to do so infuriated me. I thought being rich was a choice but that being poor certainly wasn't. In 2013, author Dave Ramsey posted an article titled "20 Things the Rich Do Every Day," written by Tom Corley.[10] It immediately went viral. A CNN blogger wrote a scathing review,[11] as did the *Huffington Post*.[12] While I may not usually agree with Dave Ramsey, I feel he and Corley got a bad rap simply for not communicating their point better—the point being to spend the free time you have investing in yourself. According to the article, being rich correlates positively with writing down goals, reading books, eating healthy and going to the gym, making to-do lists, networking, and believing in lifelong education and self-improvement. Being poor positively correlates with eating junk food, watching reality TV, waking up late, not reading, and always saying what's on one's mind.

Of course, correlation does not equal causation. Engaging in the above activities (or not engaging in them) won't make you rich or poor. However, if you really think you have no control over being rich or poor and it's all about the cards you were dealt in life, try taking the actions of rich people for a simple period of time and see how it feels. My guess is that you will feel phony at first, "pretending" to be the kind of person who networks and writes down goals you don't actually believe you can achieve—but never underestimate the power of "acting as if."

These six tips will help you, but always remember the bottom line: getting ahead financially will be challenging if you resent money and feel you have no other choice than to be in debilitating student loan debt. You should at least go through the motions of someone who enjoys money and sees it for its possibilities. Pick just one step in thinking like a millionaire. Just one. Then take that step.

Notes

1. Elkins, K. (2015, 10 October). 15 quotes from Warren Buffett that take you inside the mind of a legendary investor. *Business Insider*. https://www.businessinsider.com/warren-buffetts-greatest-quotes-2015-10.

2. Kroll, L., & Dolan, K. A. (Eds.). (2018, March 6). Meet the members of the three-comma club. *Forbes*. https://www.forbes.com/billionaires/#93cfb9d251c7.

3. All names in this book have been changed to protect privacy.

4. Gallan, J. (Producer, Director), & Rock, C. (Writer). (2004). *Never Scared* [Motion Picture]. USA: Home Box Office (HBO).

5. Powell, A. (2016, February 26). The costs of inequality: More money equals better health care and longer life. *U.S. News & World Report*. Retrieved August 28, 2018, from https://www.usnews.com/news/articles/2016-02-23/the-costs-of-inequality-more-money-equals-better-health-care-and-longer-life.

6. Wilcockson, J. (2011, February 17). Inside cycling with John Wilcockson: Armstrong's 25-year journey is over. *VeloNews*. Retrieved March 20, 2016, from https://velonews.competitor.com/2011/02/news/inside-cycling-with-john-wilcockson-armstrong's-25-year-journey-is-over_160347.

7. Deemer, A. (2009). *Solving the wealth puzzle: The rich didn't get wealthy in the stock market—you won't either!* Bloomington, IN: iUniverse.

8. Trafton, A. (2015, April 17). Study links brain anatomy, academic achievement, and family income. MIT News Office. Retrieved March 21, 2016, from news.mit.edu/2015/link-brain-to-anatomy-academic-achievement-family-income-0417.

9. Bergland, C. (2015, April 18). Why do rich kids have higher standardized test scores? *Psychology Today*. https://www.psychologytoday.com/us/blog/the-athletes-way/201504/why-do-rich-kids-have-higher-standardized-test-scores.

10. Corley, T. (2013, September 11). The Dave Ramsey Show: Interview with Tom Corley. Rich Habits. richhabits.net/dave-ramsey-rich-habits-tom-corley/.

    Note: the article on Dave Ramsey's website, "20 Things the Rich Do Every Day," has since been replaced with another, "5 Simple Habits of the Average Millionaire," possibly due to the backlash caused by the original article.

11. Evans, R. H. (2013, November 30). What Dave Ramsey gets wrong about poverty. *CNN Belief Blog*. Retrieved March 24, 2016, from religion.blogs.cnn.com/2013/11/30/what-dave-ramsey-gets-wrong-about-poverty/.

12. Irwin, B. 20 things the poor really do every day that the rich never have to worry about. (Updated 2014, January 25). In *Huffington Post*, https://www.huffingtonpost.com/2013/12/06/poverty-america_n_4398703.html, via *AlterNet*, https://www.alternet.org/20-things-poor-really-do-everyday-rich-never-have-worry-about.

CHAPTER 2

NEVER WORK FOR FREE AGAIN

T his chapter may not apply to you, as you may not have unpaid internships in your industry. Unpaid internships are often associated with creative careers like media, music, art, and fashion and don't necessarily apply to technology, medicine, or law. I spent two years doing mulitple unpaid internships in the film industry. One was OK; another involved me writing someone else's book for free and without credit; the others involved pulling twelve-plus-hour days, getting screamed at, and being forced to do the lowliest tasks with no promise of ever transitioning to paid work. None of the MBAs, technologists, engineers, or doctors I knew with six-figure student loan debt had held unpaid internships. Almost all of the arts majors I interviewed had.

Part 1: Me

I show up to the pickup point at exactly 5:30 a.m. By 5:31, I would have missed the production van and would have had to take a fifty-dollar taxi ride to the filming location.

Once I arrive on set, the unit production manager, Travis, yells at me to go get a chair out of our "holding area" two blocks away (the place we left our coats, bags, and other crap—today it's a bar that is closed during the day). I am to bring the chair to the makeup room, which is in a wedding chapel. When I ask why the makeup person can't just use one of the hundreds of chairs inside the chapel, Travis yells that they are all the wrong height.

I walk to the bar, get a giant barstool, and start half-carrying, half-dragging it down the sidewalk. Upon seeing me, one of the location managers starts screaming, "You can't remove property from its location!" I expect Travis to come to my rescue, as he is standing a few feet away—but after I explain that he demanded I transport the chair, he denies the whole thing.

I celebrate a lunch break six hours into the day by having to watch the equipment while everyone else eats and socializes (they bring me a plate of cold food thirty minutes in). I spend the last five hours of the day shivering in an alleyway, making sure nobody comes in the back door during filming, as we could not lock the door due to fire safety issues.

The whole day has been dedicated to filming an over-the-top wedding reception scene with about a hundred extras. Now, filming has finished, and I am told to help the props and locations departments clean up so we can all go. All the tables have to be stripped of the now-stale cake slices, plastic champagne flutes filled with flat apple cider, and napkins that were used for face-blotting throughout the day of shooting. Three very tired people are throwing the cake slices and used utensils into large trash bins that were dragged in earlier. The bins are already overflowing. I start picking up dirty plates and taking them over to the trash.

"What do you think you're doing!?" It's the same locations manager who yelled at me about the chairs earlier.

"I'm supposed to be helping you guys clean," I stammer.

"Those plates are the prop department's. How many times do I have to tell you: production assistants cannot touch other departments' property."

"I thought we were just throwing stuff away."

"That's because you have no clue as to what's going on."

I don't tell him that I am an unpaid intern. I am *not* one of the other production assistants, who make $85 a day to endure this abuse—though I doubt that $85 would make the situation feel much better. No one has briefed me on any set protocol at any point.

"How can I help?"

"Push down the trash so we can pack more in," he tells me.

"I thought you just said I couldn't touch the paper plates," I say. This legitimately confuses me.

"All of this stuff is the prop department's property—until it goes into the trash. Then it's trash. So get your arms in there and pack it down."

I have a master's in film production from New York University, the Harvard of film schools. How in the world are my arms shoulder-deep in trash that I am only allowed to touch *after* it crosses the elusive boundary of the bin—and I'm *not even getting paid*?

Technically, I could walk off the production any time, but I don't. Why? I need the experience on my résumé, and if I were to quit, I'd be giving up my credit in the finished film (my only compensation for this misery) and the past four weeks would become a total waste.

The production van drops everyone off at 42nd Street, across from the Port Authority bus terminal.

"See everyone at 5:30 a.m. tomorrow," Travis reminds us. I take the A train up to the 125th Street stop in Harlem, where I am couch-surfing with a friend who seems to have developed a drinking problem.

I get home at a few minutes before midnight. While checking email, I see yet another message from Sallie Mae. I know that I shouldn't open it, shouldn't kick myself while I'm down, but I ignore these instincts. I pour myself a pint glass of red wine and light a cigarette. Normally I wouldn't smoke indoors, but the place is so disgusting and my life is so depressing that it somehow seems appropriate.

With interest having rolled in at 8.5 percent for the past five years (in and out of NYU graduate school), my balance is now $286,000. I stand in the barely lit kitchen and smoke in silence, too stunned by the number to react any other way. I gulp down the red wine, wash my face, and set my alarm for 4:30 a.m.

This is my life.

Why did I take this internship? Why does *any* recent graduate take an unpaid internship? I was hoping it would lead to paid work—which, as the days go on, seems less and less likely, particularly since I learned that Travis works weekend shifts at a bakery because the work doesn't pay enough for him to survive in New York City. Like a lot of people who go into debt for their education, I went to graduate school so that this *wouldn't* be my life. I took out a lot of extra loans to study at a prestigious school, hoping the investment would pay off. But nothing paid off. In fact, it seemed I was actually worse off than if I had not gone to graduate school at all.

Many of us can look back to a time in our childhoods where we thought a good education combined with hard work would be the way to a better life. There were some years where my father supported a family of four on a $20K annual salary. We always worried about having enough money. My grandfather, a farmer who had lived through the Great Depression, told me to forget about education and focus on working instead. In retrospect, I think that was pretty good advice. However, I had a lot of ideas and plans about finding "my passion" and a career I was excited about. It seemed to me that my parents (and most of my extended family) just worked typical nine-to-fives that didn't fulfill any greater purpose. Only my uncle had money. When we went to his house in California, I marveled at how he had a house-keeper, nice cars, and (what was, to me) a mansion with a pool. That family never seemed to argue about money, and my cousin's college was completely paid for by his parents.

I got straight A's throughout high school, achieved high SAT scores, and planned to apply for top schools like Harvard and Yale. One day, around the age of seventeen, my parents sat me down for a serious conversation. They explained that Ivy League schools were way out of our budget and encouraged me to attend a state school instead. Crushed, I asked my dad why we couldn't just take out some loans so I could go. He refused. My parents would not cosign my loans or contribute more than a few thousand dollars per year for my studies. With the help of a school counselor, I found some out-of-state schools that offered tuition scholarships and got into one in California. I worked hard, but upon graduation, I found that I still didn't know what to do with my life. I wanted to make money and I had studied business, but I hated the idea of working at a bank. It seemed boring. That's when I took some more classes at a San Francisco community college and discovered a love for film.

Upon my decision to get a master's degree in film production, friends and family asked me questions like "But what are you going to do for *work*?" and "How are you going to make money?" My classmates and I all had roughly the same answer: we'd make some films, send them to some festivals, and get internships that would lead to paid work in film and television development, production, and post-production.

Between 2009 and 2010, I worked a total of three unpaid internships, none that led to paid work—not for me or any of the other interns either. I had completed two internships in Los Angeles; having been unable to find paid work there, I came to New York. I didn't just get coffee or make copies; my work ranged from mass-mailing script packets to partners and taking meeting notes to editing a book and working as a receptionist and a production assistant. The films debuted at Venice and had theatrical releases; the book sold several thousand copies. I never saw a penny.

Why did I do it? Because if I didn't, hundreds of other graduate and undergraduate film students would have. They would then "know people" in the industry, which automatically meant they *had* to be doing better than someone who didn't have any industry contacts, right?

Not necessarily. Every year, the National Association of Colleges and Employers (NACE) surveys students on whether internships either with or without some kind of compensation lead to paid jobs. Results consistently show that paid internships lead to job offers prior to graduation, whereas unpaid internships offer virtually no advantage over people with no internship experience whatsoever.[1] I imagine maybe there was a time that internships did lead to paid jobs (perhaps when the economy was better) and that's why everyone still talks about them being valuable. But I want you to be armed with the knowledge that unpaid interns generally don't fare any better than non-interns in their job searches—and I want you to promise yourself that you'll never work for free again.

In some industries like journalism, art, fashion, or film, one might argue that the only internships or entry-level jobs available are unpaid, and to some extent, that's true. As I'm writing this sentence, almost one hundred unpaid internships have posted on the New York City Craigslist "Jobs" section every day for the last five days. These industries may seem inherently evil and exploitative, but a better theory on why they continue to run on unpaid, often illegal, internships is because they are simply not performing well.

The US Bureau of Labor Statistics reports that employment in apparel manufacturing has declined by more than 80 percent since 1990.[2] In April 2018, *Variety* reported that US movie-going attendance was at its lowest in twenty-three years.[3] Magazine circulation and advertising revenue has been on the decline for years.[4] Additionally, nonprofit sectors are not held to the US Department of Labor's criteria for legal unpaid internships, and neither is the US government.[5]

Part 2: Them (a.k.a. "The One Percent")

Guess who doesn't work for free? Rich kids. Intern Bridge's 2010 survey of 27,335 students found that students from high-income families were more likely to be found in paid internships with for-profit companies, compared to lower-income students who received paid internships at a significantly lower rate and were more likely to have paid internships with nonprofits than high-income students. High-income students were less likely to be in paid internships with government agencies.[6]

Rich people learn, often from an early age, not to undersell themselves—not to offer their work for free or cheap—and it pays off. In 2014, *Forbes* magazine reported that people who have worked unpaid internships tend to take lesser-paying jobs than those with no internship experience whatsoever and are paid about a third less than counterparts who had worked paid internships.[7] According to the article, the average salary for a first job for someone having just completed an unpaid internship is $35,721, compared to $37,087 for a person with no internship experience and $51,930 for someone with paid internship experience.

The real question then becomes whether or not "rich kids" have been successful at landing paid internships in more difficult-to-access industries. Unfortunately, there is no readily available statistic or study to answer this. Logically, though, everything adds up: if someone works for free, they will likely work for lower-than-average pay; if they work for lower-than-average pay once, they'll probably *continue* to work for lower-than-average pay; if they continue working for lower-than-average pay, they'll likely struggle financially for the foreseeable future. In this light, it doesn't make sense to say, "I'll work this unpaid internship just to get my foot in the door." Such thinking could be the first step toward a lifetime of financial insecurity and struggle.

When I was working three unpaid internships, I thought, *If just one of these could lead to a connection, and paid work . . .* The bigger question should have been, *Why would I want to turn an unpaid internship into a job? If an employer can't afford to pay a small stipend for basic office work, how would they ever be able to pay me a wage that is livable and also affords me an excess that I can use to pay down my student loan debt?* What was I thinking, really? Was I going to edit a book, or answer phones, or read scripts so well for free that, all of a sudden, my employer would decide to pay $50–$60K per year for the exact same work? Face it—this makes NO sense. We don't pay a dollar for a pound of bananas at the supermarket then offer the store three dollars for a pound the next time because the last ones were so delicious. We will continue paying a dollar until we find a different shop that sells the same product for fifty cents.

The rich know that it's hard to come back once you have devalued yourself, so they don't—regardless of how qualified they may be. The irony of the whole situation is that while people from lower-income families will likely need to take out more loans for college and graduate school, they are somehow also *more likely* to work for free, thereby stamping an unfavorable debt-to-income ratio on their heads, which snowballs into more financial insecurity when they try to earn more, get lower interest rates on mortgages, or earn higher rates of return on investments. In fact, who can even think about investing when we can't even save for retirement and are stuck in six-figure student loan debt?

Wealthy people use cost-benefit analysis (CBA) to evaluate almost every decision they make, including what to study and where to work. In layman's terms, CBA is a systemic approach to estimate the strengths and weaknesses of a potential action. It sounds like an obvious and relatively simple process of asking oneself *Do the potential payoffs justify the money spent?* but anyone who attended a Business 101 class in college may remember it takes at least a week to get through learning all the steps. In general, the steps are:

1. List alternatives.
2. List stakeholders.
3. Select measurement and measure all cost/benefit elements.
4. Predict outcome of costs/benefits over a relevant period of time.
5. Convert everything to a single currency.
6. Apply a discount rate.
7. Calculate the net present value of project options.
8. Perform sensitivity analysis.
9. Adopt recommended choice.

Luckily, Money Under 30 has created an amazing online tool that does all of the math for you.[8] In a form similar to the one on the right, you can input current job information, cost of graduate school, loan details, and earning potential after school.

Let's look at two cost-benefit analyses. One involves a woman deciding whether to go to graduate school, and the other explores an unpaid internship with possible benefits for long-term career goals.

Grad school ROI calculator

To use the grad school ROI calculator, enter the details of your graduate school program and anticipated income after graduation.

Current Age	26
Current Salary	$ 35000
Expected Salary with Graduate Degree	$ 55000
Length of Graduate School Program (Years)	2
Cost of Graduate School and Living Expenses (Per Year)	$ 20000
Total Amount You'll Borrow	$ 15000
Student Loan APR	6 %
Student Loan Term (Years)	10

Hide Advanced
▲

Submit

Marian

Marian is 27 years old and stuck in a dead-end office job, earning $50,000 per year doing marketing and distribution for an organic food company. She has not received a raise since starting three years ago, but she often receives a Christmas bonus of $1000–$2000. She entered the field because she is passionate about healthy eating and natural remedies, but she feels her motivation is stifled by lengthy Excel charts and PowerPoint presentations. She considers getting a master's degree in nutrition from Boston University. The degree takes one year to complete and costs $72,811.[9]

We assume Marian will enter graduate school at age twenty-eight. She may pick up some part-time campus work but will mostly focus on school, seeing as the program is only one year long. Let's conclude she takes out $60,000 in student loans to cover the cost of school.

To calculate her post-graduation salary, Marian goes to PayScale (www.payscale.com), where she can input her exact degree, university, age, city, and other details that will calculate her market worth. If she graduates in 2019 and lives in Los Angeles, her market value will be approximately $50,306 upon graduation and she will probably increase her earnings by 4 percent every five years.

Does it make sense for Marian to go to graduate school? Will she be any better off financially in the long run? Here is Marian's CBA chart before calculations, as entered into Money Under 30's online calculator:

Grad school ROI calculator

To use the grad school ROI calculator, enter the details of your graduate school program and anticipated income after graduation.

Current Age	28
Current Salary	$ 51000
Expected Salary with Graduate Degree	$ 50306
Length of Graduate School Program (Years)	1
Cost of Graduate School and Living Expenses (Per Year)	$ 72811
Total Amount You'll Borrow	$ 60000
Student Loan APR	7.5 %
Student Loan Term (Years)	10

Here's what the calculator returns:

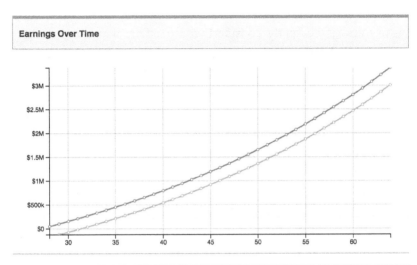

Earnings Over Time	

Lifetime Earnings	
At Current Salary	$3,374,869
At New Salary	$3,012,058
Age When Post-Grad Earnings Exceed Current Projection	N/A

The top line represents her current salary, and the bottom, her new salary. We learn that the combination of not working plus paying off the debt from graduate school means that Marian will make about $370,000 less during her lifetime than if she just stayed at the job she has.

Of course, life isn't all about money. Maybe Marian will be a lot happier in her new line of work and graduate school will have still been the right choice for her. I'm just asking you to consider what the extra $370,000 would have manifested in her life. Maybe she'd retire earlier, start a side business, or buy a beach home. Is the happiness gained by her new line of work greater than the happiness she would have in her current job?

Greg

Greg just finished graduate school after obtaining his master's in art history and is currently considering two offers: a package design-er job for a global beverage conglomerate that pays $57,000 per year or an internship at a major New York art gallery that is unpaid for the first year but guaranteed to land him a job paying $12/hour after-wards. His student loan debt currently totals $106,000. He applies for income-based payments so that regardless of which job he takes, he will only be responsible for paying 10 percent of his salary to the loans. He is thirty years old.

Some family members tell him to take the stable designer job where he will get benefits and possible long-term career growth. However, his dream is to work in a New York City gallery, and he knows that he is committed to working hard for his dream. He doesn't mind having a little less than other people so long as he's happy with what he's doing.

How will the internship affect his long-term goals? Let's look at the table to the right, which examines the lifetime earnings of both jobs (presuming a forty-hour workweek at the gallery).

The difference in him taking the internship versus the job is almost one-and-a-half million dollars in lifetime earnings. I expect this would not be casually overlooked by a wealthy person.

Of course, these are estimates. Greg could kick butt at the gallery, make some sales for a few years, make good commission. He could lose his packaging design job at the global company and not work for a year. All of that's possible. But in a likely scenario, he could earn one-and-a-half million dollars *less* by going the art gallery route. Not to mention that in the first few years, Greg's loan payments would be around $800 per month, which, after tax, would leave him with only $762 to live on every month in New York City. Why do I see a week-end job in Greg's future?

Bottom line: rich people don't plan for the most optimistic out-come; they prepare for the least optimistic one. It is pretty rare to hear someone say they wish they hadn't.

	LIFETIME EARNINGS WITHOUT INTERNSHIP			LIFETIME EARNINGS WITH INTERNSHIP	
Year	Salary	Annual Raise (%)	Year	Salary	Annual Raise (%)
1	$57,000	1.02	1	0	1.02
2	$58,140	1.02	2	$25,000	1.02
3	$59,303	1.02	3	$25,500	1.02
4	$60,489	1.02	4	$26,010	1.02
5	$61,699	1.02	5	$26,530	1.02
6	$62,933	1.02	6	$27,061	1.02
7	$64,191	1.02	7	$27,602	1.02
8	$65,475	1.02	8	$28,154	1.02
9	$66,785	1.02	9	$28,717	1.02
10	$68,120	1.02	10	$29,291	1.02
11	$69,483	1.02	11	$29,877	1.02
12	$70,872	1.02	12	$30,475	1.02
13	$72,290	1.02	13	$31,084	1.02
14	$73,736	1.02	14	$31,706	1.02
15	$75,210	1.02	15	$32,340	1.02
16	$76,714	1.02	16	$32,987	1.02
17	$78,249	1.02	17	$33,647	1.02
18	$79,814	1.02	18	$34,320	1.02
19	$81,410	1.02	19	$35,006	1.02
20	$83,038	1.02	20	$35,706	1.02
21	$84,699	1.02	21	$36,420	1.02
22	$86,393	1.02	22	$37,149	1.02
23	$88,121	1.02	23	$37,892	1.02
24	$89,883	1.02	24	$38,649	1.02
25	$91,681	1.02	25	$39,422	1.02
26	$93,515	1.02	26	$40,211	1.02
27	$95,385	1.02	27	$41,015	1.02

LIFETIME EARNINGS WITHOUT INTERNSHIP			LIFETIME EARNINGS WITH INTERNSHIP		
28	$97,293	1.02	28	$41,835	1.02
29	$99,238	1.02	29	$42,672	1.02
30	$101,223	1.02	30	$43,526	1.02
31	$103,248	1.02	31	$44,396	1.02
32	$105,313	1.02	32	$45,284	1.02
33	$107,419	1.02	33	$46,190	1.02
34	$109,567	1.02	34	$47,114	1.02
35	$111,759	1.02	35	$48,056	1.02
Lifetime	$2,849,685.23		Lifetime	$1,200,845.04	
Cost of Debt		$193,440.00	←*Assumes 7.5% interest*		
Difference in Earnings		$1,455,400.19	*with a 20-year payoff*		

Part 3: You

If you're anything like me, you have dreams and ideas about yourself and what would make you happy that numbers are not going to penetrate. Maybe you're taking all this information in and saying, "I'm different. I will be the exception to the rule. Everyone else has trouble making money in my field; I won't. Other people's unpaid internships don't lead to paid work; I will use the connections I make to find something." You might say all of these things but still have some lingering belief in your subconscious that you aren't worth getting paid because you really don't have much experience. Such thinking is what many people call a "limiting belief," and while this is not a book about limiting beliefs or thinking your way out of problems, I can say from my own experiences that (a) limiting beliefs can have real consequences in one's finances and career and (b) they often hide behind a lot of hard work, bravado, and straight-out insistence to the contrary.

If you honestly feel that you *must* intern, be prepared to ask for at least the legal minimum wage in your area. (Keep in mind that if you are not being paid, you are statistically equal to someone who has never interned, regardless of industry.) Additionally, you should receive:

- detailed direction on the activities you're assigned to,
- tasks that help you learn about the business as well as pick up specific skills needed to function in that industry or profession,
- exposure to a wide range of tasks and access to experienced people who will help broaden your skills,
- a pathway to full-time employment, or time off to attend job interviews,
- mentoring from someone at the company, and
- evaluation at the completion of the internship.[10]

Are you hearing a small voice in your head right now telling you that this advice is "unrealistic" and that I'm "out of touch"? I only ask because I would have said the same thing a few years ago. If my parents or some other adult had told me that I should ask my internship for money or detailed direction, I would have said that they "don't get how it works." They probably didn't, but that doesn't take away from the fact that I chronically undersold myself for most of my twenties. I made up a lot of reasons why I should accept what I was being offered and be happy with it. Too often, I was satisfied with earning money below my true earning potential.

A 2015 study from the University of South Carolina looked at the link between student loan debt and psychological function in twenty-five- to thirty-one-year-olds and currently enrolled students; it found that cumulative student loans were significantly and inversely associated with better psychological functioning—meaning the higher someone's loans were, the lower their behavioral, emotional, and social skills, and vice versa.[11] A 2013 study published in *Social Science & Medicine* found that high financial debt relative to available assets is associated with higher perceived stress and depression, worse self-reported general health, and higher diastolic blood pressure.[12] This shouldn't surprise anyone with student loans. However, it can be very hard to accept the feeling of letting yourself down on such a grand scale. Investing in education is essentially investing in yourself, and when the "investment" turns out to be a quarter of a million dollars of debt, it looks like the investment backfired. You look in the mirror and say to yourself, "You're a terrible investment. Investing in you ruined my life."

What kind of people or company asks a young person in debt to work for free? Probably ones that are in debt themselves, who also worked for free, who also have a hard time making ends meet. Financially successful industries (and bosses) just don't need to go there. In 2014, CNN Money published the salaries of the top twenty-five highest-paying companies for interns. Palantir, a private software company specializing in big data analysis, pays its interns a salary of $84,144 per year. Internet companies like Twitter, LinkedIn, Facebook, and Google pay between $71,628 and $81,492. Schlumberger, an oilfield services company, clocks in at the twenty-fifth position, paying its interns $55,608.[13] It's easy to see how one can work up to a six-figure salary in a few years when their internship starts at $60–$80K per year.

If, after reading all this, you still want to take a stab at interning and getting your foot in the door, that's OK. Give yourself a time limit—be it six months, one year, or two years. After that point, if your financial life still feels out of whack and it's making you unhappy, it's time to realign and prioritize your goals, giving finances a larger role in the decision-making process. Use the tools available to create cost-benefit analyses. Make choices that don't *depend* on the most optimistic outcome happening to live or retire comfortably. After all, you don't want to be working two jobs into your fifties.

Notes

1. National Association of Colleges and Employers. Type of internship experience affects job offer rates, salary. (2018, March 1). Retrieved August 23, 2018, from https://www.naceweb.org/about-us/press/2018/type-of-internship-experience-affects-job-offer-rates-salary/.

2. US Department of Labor. (2012, June). Spotlight on labor statistics: Fashion. Bureau of Labor Statistics. Retrieved May 18, 2016, from https://www.bls.gov/spotlight/2012/fashion/pdf/fashion.pdf.

3. Lang, B. (2018, April 4). Global box office hits record $40.6 billion in 2017; US attendance lowest in 23 years. *Variety.* Retrieved August 26, 2018, from https://variety.com/2018/digital/news/global-box-office-hits-record-40-6-billion-in-2017-u-s-attendance-lowest-in-23-years-1202742991/.

4. Sacks, B. (2017, July 28). What does a 16 percent decline in magazine ads mean for the industry? *Publishing Executive.* Retrieved August 26, 2018, from https://www.pubexec.com/post/16-decline-magazine-ads-mean-industry/.

5. LeCrone, L. (2013, August 15). Unpaid internships for nonprofits: Lean In joins the controversy. WayUp. Retrieved May 18, 2016, from https://www.wayup.com/guide/community/unpaid-internships-for-nonprofits-hypocritical-or-necessary/.

6. Gardner, P. (2010, January). The debate over unpaid college internships. Intern Bridge, Inc., Michigan State University. Retrieved May 16, 2016, from www.ceri.msu.edu/wp-content/uploads/2010/01/Intern-Bridge-Unpaid-College-Internship-Report-FINAL.pdf.

7. Burger, R. (2014, January 16). Why your unpaid internship makes you less employable. *Forbes.* Retrieved May 18, 2016, from https://www.forbes.com/sites/realspin/2014/01/16/why-your-unpaid-internship-makes-you-less-employable/#4b42feda7501.

8. Barret, L. (2015, December 11). Grad school ROI calculator: Is graduate school worth the cost? Retrieved September 16, 2018, from https://www.moneyunder30.com/is-graduate-school-worth-the-cost.

9. Boston University Sargent College 2018–2019 tuition and fees, www.bu.edu/sargent/admissions/graduate/financial-aid/tuition-and-fees/.

10. How to spot a good internship. (2016, February 25). SEEK Career Advice. Retrieved May 20, 2016, from https://www.seek.com.au/career-advice/how-to-spot-a-good-internship.

11. White, G. B. (2015, February 2). The mental and physical toll of student loans. *The Atlantic.* Retrieved May 26, 2016, from https://www.theatlantic.com/business/archive/2015/02/the-mental-and-physical-toll-of-student-loans/385032/.

12. Sweet, E., Nandi, A., Adam, E. K., & McDade, T. (2013, August 1). The high price of debt: Household financial debt and its impact on mental and physical health. *Social Science & Medicine, 91,* 94–100. https://www.scholars.northwestern.edu/en/publications/the-high-price-of-debt-household-financial-debt-and-its-impact-on.

13. Fox, E. J. (2014, February 28). 25 highest paying internships. CNN Money. Retrieved May 19, 2016, from https://money.cnn.com/2014/02/28/news/companies/highest-paying-internships/index.html.

CHAPTER 3

PAY LESS TAX (LEGALLY!)

I n the 2012 US presidential election, Republican candidate Mitt Romney became famous for stating that he paid 13 percent in taxes.[1] In other words, out of all the money he made, only 13 percent went to the US government. This claim made a lot of Americans angry, and it should have—particularly considering that the average American pays 14–33 percent of their income in taxes. The Mitt Romney story is hugely complicated, and the amount of tax he actually paid has been disputed by various media publications ad nauseam. So let's talk about something else—that feeling you get when you open your first paycheck at a new job, the one you managed to negotiate a small raise at, only to find that after taxes have been taken out, it really wasn't much of a raise at all.

For many people, taxes seem nonnegotiable. Yes, you can deduct small things here and there, but that never seems to take the sting out of the big chunk that disappears before you even see it. If you're anything like me, small attempts to navigate the ins and outs of paying less tax ends in frustrating and confusing web searches, where most of the advice seems like it's geared toward people who make way more money and, in general, have their lives together more.

Owing six-figure student loan debt to the US government—and watching your seven-plus-percent interest accumulate each month while knowing you could pay more if you just didn't, well, have that tax money evaporate from your paycheck—is a hard pill to swallow.

Let's look at the nuts and bolts of how paying tax is dragging out your student loan (or other debt) payoff. You probably have an idea, but we can spend another few minutes putting salt in the wound. John has a geology degree focused on oil exploration and a student loan balance of $100,000 at 7.5 percent interest, which he has paid down to $80,000. He is paying $600 per month on the balance. He takes in about $56,000 per year from working as a barista and a bartender—the only jobs he can get after the price of oil dropped last year. After taxes (assuming 20 percent), he earns approximately $1,723 every two weeks.

If John keeps making payments of $600 per month, his debt will be paid off in twenty-four years, and he will have paid $89,000 in interest. The below calculation is based on a start date of June 2018:

Current Payoff Plan	$600
Total Principal	$80,000
Total Interest	$89,318.14
Payoff Date	July 2040

Some people tell John to cancel his cable subscription, give up his gym membership, or get cheaper car insurance. He does all three and saves $120 per month, which he puts toward his debt. Now paying

$720 per month, he will be debt-free in only sixteen years and he will have paid $55,674 in interest:

Current Payoff Plan	$720
Total Principal	$80,000
Total Interest	$55,674.66
Payoff Date	**May 2032**

Most financial advisors and debt books suggest this is the best John can do, given his circumstances. He can try to find a higher-paying job, or live on less food, or downgrade his living situation further to put a few more dollars toward the debt. He can hope that one day he will be making more money and promise himself that when it happens, he will increase monthly payments on the debt to pay it off even faster.

However, if you're John, do you really want to think about being in debt for sixteen more years and throwing away $55,000 in interest? I don't. $55K could be used in much better ways: a few vacations, a down payment on a house, or a wedding. What John, his financial advisors, and his family members fail to consider is the question of *how much more* money he could pay toward the debt if less of his income immediately went to taxes.

They don't ask the question because they, like many of us, have been conditioned to think paying taxes is a nonnegotiable part of life. We don't consider the possibility of where else that tax money *could* be going because it just doesn't seem like an option. And, of course, it isn't—the money is gone before it is even cut into our paychecks. So we continue to let that happen, year after year, and learn to live on the remainder.

John currently pays $11,200 per year in taxes, if you factor in a modest 20 percent tax rate on an annual salary of $56,000. (For many people like John, the rate is closer to 30 percent.). What if there was a way for him to pay only 10 percent tax—$5,600—per year? Now his take-home pay every two weeks becomes $1,938. He puts the extra $467 every month into his student loans. His payoff timeline now looks like this:

Current Payoff Plan	$1,067
Total Principal	$80,000
Total Interest	$27,814.06
Payoff Date	**December 2024**

John will now be out of debt in only eight years and pay a total of $27,814 in interest—almost exactly half of what he pays by simply shaving down his living expenses. He is out of debt a lot faster and has over $27K more to put toward a house, retirement, or savings.

Don't feel you have to be an accounting or math expert to figure this stuff out—just go to the easy debt payoff tool at Credit Karma (creditkarma.com/calculators/debtrepayment) and plug in your current student loan balance, interest rate, and payment information to see how your numbers change over time by adding more to your monthly balance using the sliding scale.

Now, John's revelation probably seems pretty arbitrary when we consider that reducing one's tax rate from twenty to ten percent seems much more difficult than, say, picking up an Uber driving gig every now and then. And for many people, it will be. But I was *so sick* of working stupid jobs for less money than I thought I was worth while continuing to struggle and live like a college student into my twenties and thirties. I was tired of having to check my bank balance before ordering a pizza or withdrawing cash from an ATM. In other words, I was ready to hear about different options, ones that could make my debt payoff timeline radically shorter. Maybe you're at this point and maybe you're not, but I'm going to talk about some of the more extreme debt payoff strategies, just so you're aware they exist.

The quickest and easiest way to cut your taxes down to nothing (or close to it) is to simply work outside of the United States. It's certainly not the only way—we will look at many others in this chapter—but it is by far the most significant. The reason has to do with these four words: foreign earned income exclusion.

Before you start thinking of a million and one reasons why you can't move outside of the United States and never will, please understand that this completely legal thing exists called the Foreign Earned Income Tax Exclusion. Every year, the US government announces a set amount of money you can earn working abroad without having to pay *any tax* to the United States. In 2019, it was $105,900. That means that as long as you earn the US dollar equivalent of $105,900 or less in a year, the government will not demand *any* of it. This is completely legal and does not require hiring an accountant to do your taxes. It can be entered into a simple tax preparation software such as TurboTax, online.

Depending on the tax rates of the country you're working in, working abroad can free up significant portions of your income so you can put more toward your debt. Let's say you are earning the US dollar equivalent of $120,000 per year. After applying the foreign earned income exclusion of $105,900, your income is now only $14,100 as far as the US government is concerned. As of 2019, you will pay a tax rate of about 12 percent on an income of $14,100—instead of paying a tax rate of 24 percent on an income of $120,000. If you make less than the USD equivalent of $105,900 working abroad, the money may not be taxed (by the U.S. government) at all.[2]

In other words, a person making $120,000 per year in the United States will pay about $28,800 in US tax, taking home the remaining $91,200 (120,000 minus 30 percent). A person making $120,000 abroad will only pay about $1,692 in US tax, taking home the remaining $118,308—exactly $27,108 more:

> **$120,000-$105,900 = $14,100 (taxable income after applying Foreign-Earned Income Tax Exclusion)**
>
> **$14,100*.12 = $1,692 (amount of US federal tax you'll need to pay)**
>
> **$14,100-$1,692 = $12,408 (amount of income left over after paying US tax on portion that exceeded the Foreign-Earned Income Tax Exclusion)**
>
> **$12,408 + $105,900 = $118,308 (take-home pay)**

My Accidental Lightbulb Moment

I moved abroad mainly to get away from my life in the United States but discovered this added benefit along the way. I spent most of my twenties being financially challenged, and a small part of me thought that when I moved abroad, I actually could just skip filing US tax altogether. My dad informed me this was not the case. In fact, my dad *did* my taxes until I was about twenty-eight years old. One day, he told me I needed to learn how to use TurboTax and do them myself.

I logged into www.turbotax.com and created an account. It was about a thousand times easier than I expected; by simply answering questions like *Did you buy a house this year?* the website fills out all of your tax forms for you and then submits them to the IRS. Imagine my surprise when it asked, *Did you work outside of the United States this year?* and *Did you reside in a foreign country for 330 days or more?* When I answered yes to both, my entire tax bill **disappeared**.

Something must be wrong, I thought, imagining handcuffs from the FBI snapping onto my wrists the next time I visited my parents. *How can I not owe* any *tax?* But it was true, and the truth brought me from staring down a twenty-four-year timeframe for paying off my student loan debt to a mere six-year timeline. I thought I'd be paying off debt into my fifties, but instead I will likely celebrate my late thirties debt-free.

Where to Go

Don't get too excited about the prospect of not paying any taxes just yet. You may have to pay a marginal state tax depending on where you last resided, and the country you're living in will likely collect some form of income tax as well. However, if you want to target places with a low individual tax rate, consider these countries (an asterisk indicates English as an official or primary language):

- **Countries with NO income tax:** The Bahamas*, Bahrain*, Cayman Islands*, Qatar*, United Arab Emirates*, the British Virgin Islands*
- **Countries with 5 percent or less income tax:** Bosnia and Herzegovina, Guatemala
- **Countries with 0–10 percent income tax, depending on level of income:** Bulgaria, Paraguay, Kazakhstan, Macedonia, Mongolia
- **Countries with 0–15 percent income tax, depending on level of income:** Macau, Russia, Switzerland, Hong Kong*, Lithuania, the Maldives*, Sri Lanka*, Palestine, Hungary, Mauritius*
- **Countries with 0–25 percent income tax, depending on level of income:** Belarus, Cambodia, Moldova, Egypt, Estonia, Isle of Man*, Singapore*, Czech Republic, Costa Rica, Dominican Republic, Jamaica*, Nepal*, Nigeria*, Serbia, Slovakia, Trinidad and Tobago*

You might be thinking, *If I'm having difficulty finding a job, or a decent-paying job, in the United States, won't it be harder to find one in another country?* Not necessarily. One of the hardest places in the world for non-citizens to get jobs is the United States. Consequently, many Americans assume it is equally (if not more) difficult to get jobs outside of the US, as well.

Below is a table that ranks English-speaking countries by their tax rate, then shows what industries are easiest to get jobs, as well as the websites to find them. Each country's tax rate is again based on an equivalent starting salary of $70,000 per year.

All of the job-seeking websites listed on the right are in English, and I have only listed countries that only have an income tax rate less than 29 percent, i.e., countries where you would lose less money to tax than in the US.

The local labor force plays a big role in how easy you will find jobs, get a work permit, receive promotions, and extend your time abroad. Generally, the harder it is to find a local person to do your job, the more job security you have. Try your best to look for places with a labor shortage. What kinds of scenarios can create an in-country labor shortage?

- An industry is new and not a lot of local people have experience working in it (e.g., user experience, social media, advanced medicine, some tech/IT/web and media design).
- The country simply doesn't have good schools teaching a particular skill or industry, thus few people receive education in it.
- The culture doesn't value what you do, and thus attracts few locals (e.g., sales, human resources, public service).
- The job or company culture has a certain intensity or communication style that makes it difficult for locals to fit in (e.g., financial negotiations, medical, oil, construction, gaming, finance).
- Long/Early/Late hours or some other working condition that is abnormal for that culture.

COUNTRY	AVERAGE INCOME TAX RATE ←for a salary of $70K	INDUSTRIES	BEST WEBSITES FOR JOB SEARCH
Anguilla	0%	Hospitality, F+B, Infrastructure planning.	www.jobs.ai/, www.gov.ai/
Antigua and Barbuda	0%	Tourism, Web Design, Retail	Career Jet, www.caribbeanjobs.com
Bahamas	0%	Financial Services, Banking, F+B, Software development, Hospitality, Domestic Services.	242jobs.com, Linkedin, CarribeanJobs.com
Bermuda	0%	Hospitality, Domestic Services, Construction, Law, Financial Services	www.bermudajobboard.com, www.jobsinbda.com, www.bermudajobs.com, www.royalgazette.com/jobs, www.hamilton-recruitment.com/bermuda
Brunei	0%	Biomedical, Chemistry, Oil + Gas, Construction, Engineering, IT	www.jobsbrunei.com/latest-jobs/, www.brunei-da.com/brunei/jobs, www.rigzone.com/jobs/countries/BN/brunei_darussalam_jobs.asp
Cayman Islands	0%	Financial Services, Law, Administration, Tax, Compliance, Risk, IT	www.affinitycayman.com/cayman-jobs/, www.baraud.com, www.cmlor.com, www.personnel2000.com/, www.steppingsto-nescayman.com
Grenada	0%	Sales, Software Engineering,HR	www.thinkspain.com/, spain.xpatjobs.com/jobs-in/Granada, www.facebook.com/Global-Jobs-in-Granada-Spain-824797497562150/, www.thelocal.es/jobs/?-job_keyword=&job_location=Granada
Saint Kitts and Nevis	0%	Sales, Hospitality	www.sknvibes.com/ , www.inskn.com/category/business/jobs/, Search websites of international hotels in the area
UAE	0%	Almost Everything.	www.gulftalent.com/uae/jobs, www.rigzone.com/, www.dubaijobs.net/, www.naukrigulf.com/, jobs.laimoon.com/uae , uae.dubizzle.com/jobs/

COUNTRY	AVERAGE INCOME TAX RATE	INDUSTRIES	BEST WEBSITES FOR JOB SEARCH
Vanuato	0%	Agriculture, Hospitality, Engineering, Financial Services	www.wokikik.com/
Sri Lanka	0%	Media, IT, Internet, Software Engineering, Construction, Engineering	www.topjobs.lk/, www.everjobs.lk/, www.owl.lk
Singapore	4%	Finance, Marketing, Internet, Recruitment, Consulting, Advertising	Linkedin, EFinancialCareers, sg.jobsdb.com/, www.jobstreet.com.sg/
Jamaica	7%	Financial Services, Sales, IT, HR, Marketing	Linkedin, www.caribbeanjobs.com/, go-jamaica.com/, www.splashjamaica.com/
British Virgin Islands	8% (payroll tax)	Law, Compliance/ Tax, Accounting, Sales, Medical, Hospitality	www.hamilton-recruitment.com/british-virgin-islands/, www.hirebvi.com/jobs/ , www.career.vi/ , Linkedin
Israel	9%	Technology, IT, Law, Software Engineering, Sales, Marketing	Linkedin, www.jobsintelaviv.eu/, il.usembassy.gov/jobs/, www.overseasjobs.com/do/where/IL
Micronesia	9%	Domestic, Medical, Construction, Education	Craigslist Micronesia, www.fsmpio.fm/vacancy.html, www.comfsm.fm/?q=hr-jobs
Fiji	10%	Management, Engineering, Sales, Accounting, Hospitality	Linkedin, www.vacanciesinfiji.com/, www.southpacificemployment.com/fiji/, www.facebook.com/FijiVacancies/
Marshall Islands	11%	IT, Engineering, Accounting	krscareers.catsone.com/careers/, www.careerjet.com/search/jobs?l=Marshall+Islands
Niue	11%	Social Services	www.gov.nu/wb/pages/niue-public-service-commission/job-vacancies.php
Palau	11%	Education, Social Services, Police Force, Medical	palaugov.pw/job-vacancies/

COUNTRY	AVERAGE INCOME TAX RATE	INDUSTRIES	BEST WEBSITES FOR JOB SEARCH
Hong Kong	15%	Marketing, PR, Finance, Financial Services, Recruiting, Conuslting, IT, Sales, Admin + HR, Transportation, Professional Services, F+B, Education	Linkedin, hk.jobsdb.com/hk, www.indeed.hk, www.recruit.com.hk, jobs.geo-expat.com/,
Isle of Man	15%	Financial Services, Healthcare, IT, Professional Services, Insurance, Engineering,	services.gov.im, www.jobtrain.co.uk/iomgov-jobs/vacancies.aspx, www.indeed.co.uk/jobs-in-Isle-Of-Man, www.employed.im/, www.jobstoday.co.uk/, Linkedin
Mauritius	15%	Financial Services, Management, Professional Services, IT, Software Engineering, Graphic and Web Design, Recruitment, Hospitality	Linkedin, www.myjob.mu/, www.mauritiusjobs.mu/, www.careerhub.mu/,
Seychelles	15%	Hospitality, F+B	www.catererglobal.com/jobs/seychelles/, Linkedin, www.employment.gov.sc/job-opportunities/national-vacancies,
Nigeria	17%	Financial Services, Construction, Oil + Gas, Software, Telecom, Nonprofit	Linkedin, ngcareers.com/jobs, www.hotnigerian-jobs.com/, www.jobber-man.com/, joblistnigeria.com/
Ghana	18%	Financial Services, Nonprofit, IT, F+B, Web Designers, Marketing and PR, Recruiting	Linkedin, www.jobsingha-na.com, www.ghanaweb.com/GhanaHomePage/jobs/, www.ghanacurrent-jobs.com/, US Embassy Website, joblistghana.com/,
Thailand	19%	Recruitment, Hospitality, F+B, Retail, IT, Professional Services, Graphic Design, Internet, Sales	Linkedin, th.jobsdb.com/th

COUNTRY	AVERAGE INCOME TAX RATE	INDUSTRIES	BEST WEBSITES FOR JOB SEARCH
Solomon Islands	20%	Construciton, Energy, Nonprofit, Psychology	www.facebook.com/solomonislandsjobsnetwork/, unjobs.org/themes/solomon-islands
Australia	20%	Everything	Linkedin, sydneymovingguide.com/job-openings-visa-sponsorship/, www.job2go.org/jobs
Malaysia	20%	Engineering, Financial Services, Finance, IT, Digital Marketing, Sales, Accounting, Administrative	Linkedin, www.skootjobs.com/, www.jobstreet.com.my/, jobscentral.com.my/, www.bestjobs.com.my/
Malta	21%	Internet, Gaming/Casino, Administrative, Financial Services, Internet, Software Engineer,	Linkedin, jobsinmalta.com/, vacancycentre.com/jobs-in-malta/, www.reed.co.uk/jobs/malta,maltajobport.com/
Northern Ireland	21%	IT, Engineering, Accounting, Finance, Manufacturing, Construction. Software Engineering, Sales	www.nijobs.com/, www.reed.co.uk/jobs/northern-ireland, www.nijobfinder.co.uk/
Pakistan	21%	Management, IT, Medical, Textiles, Manufacturing, Pharmaceuticals, Security	Linkedin, new.brightspyre.com/, www.rozee.pk/, jobs.un.org.pk/, www.mustakbil.com/
Canada	21%	Everything.	Linkedin, ca.indeed.com/US-Citizen-Canadian-Citizen-jobs, ca.usembassy.gov . Also check jobs.goabroad.com/search/canada/jobs-abroad-1 for more resources.
Dominica	22%	Banking, Education, good for Entrepreneurs.	www.dominica.gov.dm/vacancies, www.higheredjobs.com/international/search.cfm?CountryCode=58, Linkedin (limited)

COUNTRY	AVERAGE INCOME TAX RATE	INDUSTRIES	BEST WEBSITES FOR JOB SEARCH
Suriname	22%	Geology/Mining, Software Engineering, HR, Law	www.caribbeanjobs.com/Suriname, Linkedin (Limited), www.surgold.com/jobs/, www.limapolawfirm.com/recruitment
Botswana	23%	Banking, Construction, Mining, Health, Engineering	www.careerpoolbotswana.com/, www.careersinafrica.com/l/botswana/, www.careers24.com/jobs/lc-botswana/
Lesotho	23%	Medical, Mining, Education, Nonprofit	unjobs.org/duty_stations/msu, lesothojobs.blogspot.sg/, Linkedin (Limited), www.nul.ls/index.php?option=com_content&view=category&id=59&Itemid=511
Austria	24%	Software engineering, Retail, Pharmaceuticals, Biotech, Automotive, IT, Graphic Design, Finance	www.thelocal.at/, austriajob.info/, Linkedin, www.jobsinvienna.com/
American Samoa	25%	QA, Medical	www.indeed.com/q-Jobs-l-American-Samoa-jobs.html
Belize	25%	Generally there are not many jobs for foreigners in Belize.	www.careerjet.com/search/jobs?l=Belize, www.bz.undp.org/content/belize/en/home/operations/jobs.html, Linkedin
Saint Helena	25%	Infrastructure, Accounting, General	www.sainthelena.gov.sh/vacancies/, www.saint.fm/st-helena-independent-20140829-2/
Trinidad and Tobago	25%	Sales, Accounting & Finance, Retail, IT, Business Services, Administrative	www.caribbeanjobs.com/Trinidad-and-Tobago, www.trinidadjob.com/latest-jobs.html, www.jobstt.com/, www.nestle.tt/careers
Gibraltar	26%	Accounting, IT, Insurance, Marketing and PR, Sales, Banking, Web Design, HR and Recruiting, Administration	www.recruitgibraltar.com/, Linkedin, www.indeed.co.uk/jobs-in-Gibraltar, www.thinkspain.com/jobs-in-spain/23,

COUNTRY	AVERAGE INCOME TAX RATE	INDUSTRIES	BEST WEBSITES FOR JOB SEARCH
India	27%	IT, Administrative, Internet and Techniology, Engineering (all types), Outsourcing/Offshoring, Medical, Recruitment, Banking and Financie, Professional Services, Defense.... almost everything really.	Linkedin, www.naukri.com/, www.placementindia.com/
Namibia	27%	Sales, Banking, Chemicals and Mining, Professional services, Engineering, Medical	www.namibiaatwork.gov.na/, Linkedin, www.careers24.com/jobs/lc-namibia/, eliteemployment.com.na/,
Samoa	27%	Law, Public Service, Finance, Education, IT	www.psc.gov.ws/, southpacificemployment.com/samoa/index.cfm
Zimbabwe	27%	Medical, Telecom, Accounting, Finance, Agriculture, Sales, Marketing and PR,	jobszimbabwe.co.zw/, www.recruitmentmatters.co.zw/, www.zimbabwehumancapital.org/, unjobs.org/duty_stations/hre,
Cook Islands	28%	Sales, Mining, Education, Hospitality	www.cookislandsjobs.com/, www.education.gov.ck/, www.southpacificemployment.com/

It may sound difficult to identify places with labor shortages when you're searching for jobs abroad from your home country, but most expatriates (i.e., foreign people living in that country) have some awareness of the local labor force. Many countries have online expat communities or Facebook groups, or you can connect with expats on LinkedIn in your industry, working in the country you're interested in moving to.

Getting Work Permits

Becoming legally authorized to work in a foreign country seems a daunting prospect to most. We all know what it's like applying for jobs in the US—at the end of almost every application is that final question, "Are you legally authorized to work in the US?" This is largely because the work visa required for non-Americans to work in the US can take up to a year or more to obtain—probably longer than most employers are willing to wait.

This is not necessarily the case in other countries, where the process for getting a work visa can be both easier and faster. When browsing for jobs abroad, you can assume you're okay to apply unless the post specifically says foreigners will not be considered. Some countries have salary minimums applicable for work permits, as in, a company may only be able to apply for a work permit for a "skilled" labor position, paying at least, for example, $65,000 per year; if you can make more post-tax income in the U.S., it wouldn't make sense to move.

Do you have a highly specific or specialized degree or experience? You may not even need to physically be in the country to apply. For specialized roles in industries like health care, oil drilling, geology, defense, technology, or finance, employers are likely just looking for the best person and may even be willing to pay for your relocation.

For other positions, being physically present to start work as soon as your work visa comes through can trump qualifications, particularly for desperate companies who have had openings for long periods of time. Not only are you already there, you already have experience in the local culture . . . a double win! While slightly riskier, it's totally plausible for good pre-planning plus a multi-week visit to that country to result in job prospects, thus pushing you towards your Foreign-Earned Income deduction even faster.

Making the Leap

If anything I've said here has started to convince you that moving abroad might be the best strategy for paying off significant debt, you're probably wondering, "What next? How do I find a job abroad without going into yet more debt in the process?" It's easy. Follow this simple strategy:

#1—Pick an English-speaking country with a low tax rate and jobs in the industry you work in.

(If you speak another language well, review country income tax rates for places that speak that language and then check local job-seeking websites to see if there are any openings for what you do.) Make sure it is a country that seems like a place you could see yourself living for a year or more, based on weather, culture, etc. Be realistic about the components you need to be happy. If you love skiing, don't look for jobs on the equator. You are about to embark on an exciting new chapter of your life while paying off a huge amount of debt, and the thought should be both invigorating and a tad scary.

#2—While you are still in your home country (likely working and continuing to earn money), apply for jobs from abroad.

Aim for a minimum number you will apply for before giving up – say, fifty. Ask or pay someone to give your resume a professional go-over, to ensure it is at its best before starting. Go on LinkedIn and find other people working in that country, maybe even at companies that interest you. Ask for tips on finding jobs there. Look online for expat/expatriate groups in that country and reach out to the moderator for tips on finding work.

#3—If no companies get back to you for interviews, don't despair. Save some money and plan a visit.

If you can manage to save up enough money for a one-way flight and a month of living expenses, go for a month and commit to spending each day looking for work in that country while living cheaply in an AirBnb or similar. If you are not in a place to leave your current job, save up some vacation time and go for a 9-day trip (leaving on a Friday, coming back two Sundays later). Pre-plan the trip so that you have a specific plan of job-finding attack when you are there. Meet with the contacts you made on LinkedIn and the expat groups. Forget sightseeing completely—you can do that once you live there.

Maybe moving to another country just isn't an option for you. I get it. We'll next look at some other ways you can reduce your tax burden without leaving home.

De-Mystifying Tax Deductions

My major takeaway from researching and writing this chapter is just how unnecessarily complex the US tax system is. Our policymakers have made it *so complicated* to navigate doing our own taxes that most of us just end up paying as quickly or painlessly as possible then forgetting about it as fast as we can—which, to say the least, is pretty frustrating. It is not a system that works for the majority of Americans. It mainly works for people who can afford to employ professional tax preparers.

One trap I used to fall into was thinking, *Since I barely make any money, my tax situation is simple.* I thought I didn't really need to understand much because most of the "tricks" for paying lower tax were for people a lot richer than me—people with assets, investments, multiple bank accounts, and so forth. For non-tax gurus, the advice in every direction seems to be the same: put money in your company's 401(k) or start an IRA, Roth IRA, HSA, or similar. For the longest amount of time, I thought these were my only options to pay less tax legally.

Now I know there are other options.

As mentioned earlier, you don't have to be a tax whiz as long as you have about $60 to invest in TurboTax's Deluxe edition, which helps you answer simple questions that maximize your tax savings and allow you to file your taxes online. Literally anyone could answer these, as many require a simple "yes" or "no," such as "Do you have health insurance through your job?" or "Do you own a business?"

Deductions are automatically applied, then your taxes are submitted online and your tax refund is transferred to your bank account about three weeks later.

Here are some additional suggestions on how to save money on tax without having to leave the United States at all:[3]

1. Move to a more tax-friendly state.

The first and most important thing to remember about US taxes is that what you call "your money" makes a big difference in the taxes you pay. Money that counts as "income" is taxed the most, whereas "business income" and "capital gains" are taxed less. The best way to save on income tax is to simply move to a state that doesn't have state income tax. These states are Alaska, Florida, Nevada, South Dakota, Texas, Washington, and Wyoming. You could also move to a more tax-friendly state. Texas and New Hampshire don't tax income but have higher property tax rates. Tennessee has no state income tax either but has higher sales tax rates.[4]

2. Take advantage of company-offered incentives, such as 401(k)s, Health Savings Accounts (HSAs), Flexible Savings Accounts (FSAs), or childcare reimbursement programs.

Find out from your company's human resources department what options exist. 401(k)s will take some of your pre-tax income and save it for retirement, and HSAs/FSAs will allow you to use pre-tax income toward medical expenses. Childcare reimbursement programs generally involve you paying pre-tax money into an account and then getting reimbursed later.[5]

3. Set up a home office.

If you use part of your home regularly and exclusively for operating a small business, you can deduct home office expenses such as parts of your utility bills, insurance premiums, and home maintenance bills.

One common misconception with this method is that you need to have an entire room of your residence dedicated to the home office. As of 2018, the IRS allows you to claim a standard deduction of $5 for every square foot of office space, up to 300 square feet. To be clear, this deduction only applies to you if you're self-employed and not if you simply work from home for your usual employer.[6]

4. Deduct student loan interest.

As of 2019 tax law, you can still deduct up to $2,500 of the interest paid to student loans directly from your taxable income as long as you don't exceed the adjusted gross income threshold.[7]

5. Deduct losses from federally declared disasters.

If you suffered monetary loss during a federally declared disaster (i.e., floods, hurricanes, etc), casualty losses are deductible.[8]

6. Deduct medical expenses over 10 percent of adjusted gross income.

If you pay more than 10 percent of your adjusted gross income to medical expenses, you can deduct unreimbursed, allowable medical care expenses that exceed 10 percent of your adjusted gross income.[9]

7. Incorporate a business and ask your employer to employ you as an independent contractor.

I already know what you're thinking . . . this sounds extremely awkward, uncomfortable, and unlikely. But it's worth mentioning for the sheer amount of money you can save. It is easiest for careers that don't require licensure. Instead of working in marketing, you can be an "independent marketing consultant." You set up a business but continue doing your regular job. Suddenly your income is business income and taxed at a lower percentage. If your business is a sole proprietorship or S corporation, you will get a 20 percent qualified business income deduction. If your taxable income is less than $157,000 for individuals or

$315,000 for married taxpayers filing jointly, your deduction is generally 20 percent of the net income of your business. So if your business's taxable income was $100,000, then after the 20 percent deduction, you only have to pay taxes on $80,000.[10]

8. Get a credit for being energy smart.

Energy efficiency credits are available for certain expenses you incur to upgrade your home. Qualifying solar electric, solar water heating, geothermal heat pump, or wind energy property expenses are eligible for a credit of up to 30 percent, with limits based on the capacity of some systems. The 2018 tax reform extended these credits through 2021.[11]

9. Save on sales tax by taking advantage of low- or no-sales-tax states as well as state tax holidays.

If you have any upcoming plans to travel, check your destination state's sales tax policies. Five states do not have any sales tax: Alaska, Delaware, Montana, New Hampshire, and Oregon.[12] In addition, some states offer sales-tax-free shopping on food, clothing, or over-the-counter drugs.

Additionally, as of 2019, seventeen states offer certain weekends of sales-tax-free shopping. The rules vary per state—sometimes there is a price cap of $75–$100 in order to qualify for the tax deduction; sometimes it's limited to clothing and shoes. Check your state for more details. Participating states are: Alabama, Arkansas, Connecticut, Florida, Iowa, Maryland, Massachusetts, Mississippi, Missouri, New Mexico, Ohio, Oklahoma, South Carolina, Tennessee, Texas, Virginia, and Wisconsin.[13]

If none of these scenarios is feasible for you to save money on taxes, don't despair. Not every suggestion in this book will work for everyone. The point is that you start challenging your existing beliefs about money, debt, tax obligation, and how the world works. Remember: "You must learn the rules before you break them. . . . Genius is far rarer than people think."[14]

Notes

1. Finnegan, M., & Abcarian, R. (2012, August 16). Romney says his tax rate was at least 13% in last 10 years. *Los Angeles Times*. Retrieved June 18, 2016, from articles.latimes.com/2012/aug/16/nation/la-na-romney-taxes-20120817.

2. Erb, K. P. (2018, March 7). New: IRS announces 2018 tax rates, standard deductions, exemption amounts and more. *Forbes*. https://www.forbes.com/sites/kellyphillipserb/2018/03/07/new-irs-announces-2018-tax-rates-standard-deductions-exemption-amounts-and-more/#363d32bb3133.

3. *Kiplinger's Personal Finance* editors. (2018, August 10). 14 ways for everyone to save on taxes under the new tax law. Kiplinger. Retrieved September 14, 2018, from https://www.kiplinger.com/slideshow/taxes/T054-S011-ways-for-everyone-to-save-on-taxes-under-the-new-t/index.html.

4. Loudenback, T. 2018, Apr 13. The 9 places in the US where Americans don't pay state income taxes. *Business Insider*. https://www.businessinsider.com/no-income-tax-states-2018-2.

5. California Department of Human Resources. (Updated 2016, October 4). Dependent Care. CA.gov. Retrieved September 14, 2018, from www.calhr.ca.gov/employees/Pages/reimbursement-accounts-dependent-care.aspx.

6. IRS Small Business and Self-Employed website. (Updated 2018, May 1). Home office deduction. Internal Revenue Service. Retrieved September 14, 2018, from https://www.irs.gov/businesses/small-businesses-self-employed/home-office-deduction.

7. IRS Tax Topics. (Updated 2018, January 31). Topic number 456—Student loan interest deduction. Internal Revenue Service. Retrieved September 14, 2018, from https://www.irs.gov/taxtopics/tc456.

8. Personal casualty & theft loss deductions severely limited. (2018, February 1). SC&H Group. Retrieved September 14, 2018, from https://www.schgroup.com/resource/blog-post/2018-tax-roadmap-personal-casualty-theft-loss-deductions-severely-limited/.

9. Bunis, D. (2018, January 12). How you can deduct your medical expenses. AARP Money. Retrieved September 14, 2018, from https://www.aarp.org/money/taxes/info-2018/medical-deductions-irs-fd.html.

10. 2018 tax reform details: 5 big wins for small business owners. (n.d.). Wealth Factory. Retrieved September 16, 2018, from https://wealthfactory.com/articles/2018-tax-reform-details-5-big-wins-for-small-business-owners/.

11. Caplinger, D. (2018, March 23). 19 tax hacks for 2018. The Motley Fool. Retrieved September 14, 2018, from https://www.fool.com/slideshow/19-tax-hacks-2018/?slide=20.

12. Moreno, T. (Updated 2018, November 6). The 5 US states without a statewide sales tax. The Balance. Retrieved September 14, 2018, from https://www.thebalance.com/states-without-a-sales-tax-3193305.

13. Tuttle, B. (2018, Aug 3). Sales tax holidays are back. *Time* Money. time.com/ money/5356365/tax-free-weekend-sales-tax-holidays-2018/.

14. Collins, J. P. (1921). The standards of English music: A talk with Mr. Edward German. *The Bookman, 60,* 186–8.

CHAPTER 4

BUYING PROPERTY WHEN YOU HAVE DEBT

After my long journey through debt, I staunchly believe paying rent is akin to lighting hard-earned dollars on fire and watching the tiny pieces of ash disappear into the wind like snow. You wouldn't do this with your cash, so don't do it any other way either.

There are two situations in which you *should* pay rent:

1. When you can get such a good deal on rent due to rent control, a work subsidy, etc. that it results in the rent being considerably less than a mortgage payment—*and* you can still afford to save money in other ways to make up for the fact that you are not contributing to your own net worth when paying for the roof over your head.

2. When you live in a place where the housing market is grossly overinflated and prices are likely to drop or crash in the next

few years. This is sort of a matter of opinion, but some say signs of a potentially overpriced housing market are that the increase in housing prices over time is more than the increase in income or economic growth for that area in the same period of time, making a monthly mortgage payment much more expensive than a rent payment in the same area.

For example, I know of a guy who lives in the Tribeca neighborhood of New York City in a two-thousand-square-foot industrial loft space that is basically the upstairs of his ground-level office. He writes off the entire rental as a business expense, minus $1,000, which he contributes as personal rent for the upstairs space. Did I mention he started the lease over a decade ago? If he ever moved to a similar apartment or bought a similar property in a comparable neighborhood, he could expect to pay upwards of $10K per month for either rent or a mortgage. Any time you can swing a deal like this, you should. You're winning.

As of 2014, 11 million Americans spent half or more of their income on rent, and 21.3 million spend at least 30 percent on rent.[1] Are you one of them? Consider the lunacy in making rent and student loans some of your top two outgoing expenses. It is choosing an eternity of working hard while never having anything to show for your hard work—specifically convenience, comfort, or luxury.

Common Misconceptions about Buying Property

What if paying rent is not something you in fact have to do but something you've *convinced* yourself you have to do? When talking to people with a lot of student loan debt (and/or other consumer debt), I often hear excuses. I believe these excuses are driven by fears of failure and discomfort, as well as a lack of understanding on the property-buying process. I used to smoke cigarettes and know from that experience that fear of discomfort during quitting and fear of failing is what keeps people smoking—*not* that they are lazy, dumb, and have no regard for their health. I had many of these same justifications for not buying a house, but after taking the plunge, I realized my fears were unfounded. Here are some common misconceptions about buying a house—do any sound familiar?

Misconception #1: I don't know if I'm going to live here forever, so it seems like a bad idea.

This is kind of like saying, "I don't know if I'll die by being hit by a bus, so in the meantime I'll just smoke, eat lard, and never wear sunscreen."

Wasting money is wasting money. When you pay rent, you know with 100 percent certainty that money is gone and never coming back. When you pay into a mortgage, you know that the money will likely, in some form, return. It may not *all* return—the market could go south, there could be some huge repair or a natural disaster that you need to put more money into to fix, or some other circumstance may force you to quickly sell it off for less money than you paid.

Let's say you buy a $200,000 house in which the monthly mortgage payment is $1,500 per month. You put only 3 percent down to buy the house ($6,000) and your mortgage loan is $194,000. You pay the mortgage for a year and then decide to get married and sell the house. It would probably be better in this scenario to rent out the house to continue building equity, but let's assume you are strapped for cash and that's not an option.

You sell the house for $190,000—$10K less than what you paid for it. Your mortgage loan at this point is $176,000, since you have paid off $1,500 every month. After paying off the mortgage with the money from the sale, you pocket $14,000 to put toward your new house. Considering the $6,000 you put in when you bought the house, your profit is still $8,000. This does not factor in interest and depreciation, but you get the idea. If you spent money on home improvements, you would presumably be able to sell it for a little more than what you paid, recouping the money.

Had you rented an apartment for $1,500 a month instead, you would simply be $18,000 poorer.

Misconception #2: I can't get a mortgage with my credit and other debt.

Perk up, Debbie Downer. Have you been denied on more than five mortgage applications? No? So how do you know?

You may be right—perhaps your debt-to-income ratio is not right for you to get a mortgage at this time. But you may learn that there are more options than you realize—different types of home financing options that are available for your specific situation. This research will be done for free by the mortgage broker you're going to hire. This person will become your champion and ally in the home-buying process and will write you offers on Sunday nights after receiving five frantic text messages from you about whether you can afford some properties you saw at an open house that afternoon. The mortgage broker is not out to take your money. He or she only makes money once you buy something. Get on Yelp and find your new best friend (more on this in the next section).

In short, put in a little legwork to get rejected before jumping to conclusions. Don't take yourself out of the running—let a mortgage broker do that instead. At the very least, you'll learn what you need to do to eventually purchase property and can demystify the black hole of fear surrounding the topic.

Misconception #3: I can't afford a down payment now nor can I save for one.

I had always heard you had to put 20 percent of the purchase price down in cash to buy a house. I thought that was the "standard." It is not anymore.

While it is always preferable to put down more money to get the lowest mortgage interest rate possible, people are in different situations when it comes to on-hand cash.

If you are in the military, a veteran, or a farmer, there are special types of mortgages for you that require *no* money down. If you have decent credit, you can look for what is called a private mortgage insurance (PMI) to get a mortgage with only 3 percent of the home purchase price down. If you have really bad credit and no money, you can get a Federal Housing Administration (FHA) loan. It requires a 3.5 percent down payment on the purchase price of the home, so if the purchase price is $100,000, you need to put down $3,500. That said, there are downsides to FHA loans: the terms are not as favorable and not all houses will sell to buyers financing with FHA loans. Again, this is not for you to worry about now. Let your mortgage broker worry.

Misconception #4: Buying a house is so complicated. I have no idea what kind of mortgage to even apply for.

We have already established that buying a house is not actually complicated. After you find your mortgage broker, you will need to find a real estate agent. Contact one or two. Many people might advise you to work with several realtors at once to "play the field," but I prefer to find one I really like and have them do everything. I don't have time to manage multiple relationships and make numerous people believe I am going to buy from them. My real estate agent in LA spent every single weekend (and some weeknights) driving me all over creation looking at different properties and became one of my first friends in town. It is going to be a stressful period, so pick someone you can stand and possibly even look forward to spending time with.

Misconception #5: It's such a big deal/ I don't have time.

Buying property is actually *not* that big of a deal. It is not getting married. It is not having a kid. It's a simple transaction, only slightly more complicated than taking out your student loans. The complication comes from thinking you have to do everything yourself instead of leaning on the people you assemble as your "team," namely your mortgage broker and real estate agent. They do most of the work; you fill out some paperwork, transfer some money, and look at the properties.

There is really no guesswork. You can only afford what your mortgage broker tells you is affordable for your situation, and you can only see places that fall at or under that number.

This is not to say it's not time consuming or that the decision-making process won't be stressful. You will find yourself losing sleep over decisions such as whether an extra bathroom is worth a forty-minute commute. You will want to talk these through with friends and family members who may be able to point out things you aren't thinking of and even take them to the properties you're considering.

Like everyone, you're probably busy, and the thought of doing all this work is pretty daunting. That's OK. It is less stressful than turning sixty and realizing you have no assets and will have to work forever.

Misconception #6: I'm waiting until the market changes.

OK, what do you even know about "the market"? Are you an economist? Unless you know for a fact that you can rent and still save more money than you would if you had bought a house, paid part of a mortgage, and sold it for less, this is just another excuse. Of course, do your research. If a freeway is being built outside your backyard in a year, make sure this is accounted for in the price. But for the most part, try not to worry about it. People who bought homes in 2007 only to watch the value decrease during the economic crash just stayed in their homes for another few years. Ten years later, their homes may be worth the same as what they were in 2007—but the house is now half paid off, and when they move and sell their property, they will get a fat check, something that definitely won't happen when you leave your rented place.

Misconception #7: Owning a house is expensive.

This concern actually has some validity. When something breaks or needs updating, it's you (not your landlord) who has to cough up the money to fix it. I have actually read about some people who were living paycheck to paycheck while paying off their student loans and rented solely for the ability to control their living costs completely.

I am no home-improvement expert, so I had to spend a little more on my condo to have a place that was move-in ready. If you or your partner can do home repairs or you live in an area where contractor work is reasonable, this should not be a big concern.

The first time I purchased a property, the hot water heater broke down in the third month of ownership, costing me over $2,000 to replace (the high cost had something to do with the difficulty of getting to where it was installed). It was an unexpected cost that stung for a few months. What I learned from that experience was that I had to keep a few thousand dollars in an emergency fund (which I did with www.betterment.com, where you can move money in and out without penalty while getting returns much higher than in a regular bank) so that I could pull money out easily when I needed it. Having a small emergency fund for unforeseen home costs is an easy way to counter this concern.

Misconception #8: I want to wait until [I get married/I have kids/my parents retire] before buying a house.

I understand this ambition. But I have heard a lot of people say that events like having kids or meeting one's future spouse happen when they least expect it, so I don't really get the point of waiting for something totally unknown and throwing away thousands on rent in the meantime.

Misconception #9: Nobody in my debt situation can own property.

This sounds like your fear talking. A more factual statement could be, "Nobody in my debt situation can save $100,000 for a housing down payment in any reasonable amount of time." That may be true. But maybe you don't need to.

Fannie Mae has a few options that could make home ownership more accessible to people with student debt:

1. Student Loan Cash-Out Refinance

This is an option for people who have high-interest student loans and already own a house. In many scenarios, your mortgage rate will be lower than student loan interest rates. Fannie Mae will let you pull out the money you paid toward your lower-interest-rate house and use it to repay your higher-interest student loans. For example, if you have $100,000 in student loans but have a home that you own and have paid $30,000 toward the mortgage, you can pull out the $30,000 and use it to pay off your student loans. Of course, you will now have to repay the $30,000 on your mortgage, so this really only makes sense if your mortgage has a much lower interest rate than your student loans. Details can be found on the Fannie Mae website.

2. Debt Paid by Others

In most cases, any debt that is in your name and attached to your social security number (such as student loans, credit card debt, auto loans, etc.) shows up when you are being evaluated for a mortgage. If you don't make very much money, your debt-to-income ratio may not be good enough to get a mortgage. But under this option, Sallie Mae evaluates eligibility to qualify for a home loan by *excluding* any non-mortgage debt (e.g., credit cards, auto loans, and student loans) from your debt-to-income ratio if the debt is being paid by someone else (such as a family member, employer, or friend)—even though the debt is in your name and connected to your social security number. You will need to prove that you are eligible for your employer's student loan payoff program or show that your family is taking care of payments.

3. Student Debt Payment Calculation

If you have been making payments on your student loans, Sallie Mae will now count these payments toward increasing your credit score.

Now, it might make more sense to say, "Nobody in my *credit* situation can own property," because if you have bad credit, you probably won't be able to get a mortgage. Bad credit is sort of the kiss of death with regards to property purchase, but it can be mitigated by getting a co-signer, increasing your down payment, or following the steps I outline in Chapter 6, which are free and possible to do by yourself.

I can't emphasize the importance of good credit enough. It is a cornerstone of refinancing your loans and increasing your net worth by acquiring assets (namely, property). If you have bad credit or don't know much about the state of your credit at all, we will cover this in Chapter 6.

Misconception #10: I don't want to be tied down.

My brother's favorite excuse! You might get a job elsewhere or settle down in another state, city, or country. I get it. By now you should be convinced that the property-buying process is less complicated than you may have thought previously, and guess what? So is the property-selling process.

If being "tied down" (or buying a place that you aren't sure you'll stay in) is a concern, you have one task: make sure the monthly mortgage you'll have to pay is equal to or less than rents you could charge in that area. If you have to leave town quickly for a job, you will simply need to find a property management company (Yelp is great for this) to rent out your place and collect the money you will then use for your mortgage payment while you look for a buyer. Sure, you may lose a few hundred bucks a month in management fees that you won't see again, but remember, rent that you pay equals money you *definitely* won't see ever again.

How to Buy a House

When I first got out of graduate school and I was living on a few hundred dollars per month after paying rent and my student loans, the idea of buying a house brought me a lot of pain because it just seemed impossible. Thinking about how I would probably never be able to own a house or condo made me bitterly sad and angry, and it was a topic I couldn't even talk about with my parents or partner without getting very upset and emotional. I honestly believed that I had failed and this goal was completely out of reach.

Today I own not one condo but two. I am still paying off student loan debt, but the total value of my properties will be over $600,000 once paid off. I am paying one mortgage, and a tenant who is renting my other property pays the other.

Get ready, because I'm going to tell you every single thing you need to know about how to do this. The three components of being able to buy a property are:

1. A little bit of cash
2. A decent income
3. Decent or good credit

If you just said to yourself, "I have none of those," no problem. I will tell you how to get them. (You are likely overestimating how much cash you need and how good your credit has to be anyhow.)

The bar for a *little* cash, a *decent* income, and *decent* or *good* credit is lower than you think. I used to assume these three factors affected my ability to buy any property, but what they actually affect is how low of an interest rate you can get on your mortgage—*not* whether you can buy at all.

Let's look at the two properties I own. The first is in Minnesota. A few years back I bought a condo for $105,000 in an area I grew up in. The area is very conveniently located and has always had a rental shortage, I think because people marry younger and usually buy property right away.

I rent the property out for $1,100/month; the mortgage costs $540/month, and I have to pay $150/month in homeowner's association fees (that go toward maintaining the grounds and facilities) and $90/month for the property management company (that collects rent and takes care of tenant concerns). I did put down 20 percent for this property because I had just gotten a bonus at my finance job, but let's presume I did not have any cash lying around at that point. If I had an FHA loan, I would have been required to put down 3.5 percent as a down payment—in other words, only $3,675. I would have needed about another 3 percent in cash to go toward closing costs ($3,150). To buy that property, I would need about $6,825.

If you live in an area where you pay around $1,100 in rent per month, you could likely purchase a house for a little under $7,000. That equates to saving up $350 per month for twenty months. If you can save even more, say $700 per month, you can achieve your purchase price in only ten months.

You might research FHA loans and read all kinds of things about them: sellers don't like them, the interest is higher, and so forth. But these things are not your problem. You don't have to learn about loans or become a loan expert. Your real estate agent (who gets paid by the seller, not you) will find properties that are open to buyers paying with FHA loans, and your mortgage broker (whom you can easily find on Yelp) will figure out how to get you the loan. You actually don't need to be that smart at all; you literally just do what they tell you. Visit the properties your real estate agent shows you and send the mortgage broker whatever bank statements and paystubs he or she asks for.

Maybe you live in an area that isn't so affordable. The second condo I own is in Los Angeles. I bought it for $505,000. Los Angeles is a bit of a different animal. Being that it's such a large place, it is possible to rent for a large range of prices in a variety of scenarios. If you're open to living with roommates or in a tiny studio, it is possible to find something for $1,000–$1,800/month, but it won't be anywhere you can probably entertain or feel confident taking a date home. I personally don't like the idea of doing that in my thirties or forties, though I would have thought nothing of it in my twenties.

There's something that feels so unforgiving about living somewhere that makes no testament whatsoever to your hard work over the years and serves as a daily reminder of financial failure. Yet we are told to do this constantly by most "get out of debt" resources. I'm sure you've read many stories of people who lived in a container, or a moving van in the parking lot of their work, and so forth. It sounds so easy, right? Just live in a dump and get out of debt. I personally feel this is absolutely the worst kind of advice around. Living like a homeless college dropout not only amplifies your sense of guilt and shame over your debt but it chips away at any remaining self-worth you have.

Consider the cumulative effect on our psyche when we don't value ourselves. Personally, I've spent a lot of time living in a way where I treated myself worse than I'd treat someone I didn't like, and I've spent other years treating myself as I would treat my boss, a guest, a role model, or anyone else I highly regard. I am more successful doing the latter.

So *ignore* the debt books that tell you to eat tuna salad for dinner every night and drive a crappy car and live in a crappy apartment. Stop doing all of these things now. You are better than this. Buy a house and fill it with secondhand designer furniture from Chairish or Craigslist. Never step foot in IKEA again. I want this life for you, and by the time you've finished reading this book, I hope to have convinced you that you deserve it.

Now, you may be saying, "This all sounds great, but where do I start?" Here's exactly what you need to do:

Step 1: Find a mortgage broker.

If you are thinking, *Don't I need to find a house I like before I find a mortgage broker?* my answer is a resounding *No*. Find your broker before you look at a single property, because it will encourage good real estate agents to work with you and show you the best properties.

Go to Yelp (www.yelp.com) and search for "mortgage broker" in your city. Regardless of where you live, a lot of companies will come up. Rank by rating and click on some of the people with 4.5- or 5-star reviews, then start reading what other people have written about them. What you want to see are *recent* reviews by people who rave about how the mortgage broker was kind and courteous, did honest and efficient work, and found great rates.

Get in touch with one or a couple of these brokers. You need to tell them how much you are currently making, how much cash (if any) you can put toward a down payment, and where you are looking to buy (neighborhood preferences, etc.). After answering a few questions, your mortgage broker should be able to tell you your budget and write up a preapproval letter that simply says they can get you the funding to afford a property for that price. This entire process takes between a day and maybe a week.

Nine out of ten people shopping for real estate don't have preapproval letters. You have one because you probably don't have much money to put down and you won't be shopping for the most expensive properties, so this letter shows real estate agents that it is safe to work with you and show you properties.

Step 2: Find some properties online that you want to view.

Now that you know your budget, start your shopping online. Some sites I like are:

- Redfin (www.redfin.com)
- Trulia (www.trulia.com)
- Realtor.com
- Homes.com
- Open Listings (www.openlistings.com)
- Zillow (www.zillow.com)

Do a search by budget, and then brace yourself—if you live in an expensive area or a big city, you might find that what you can afford limits you to less-than-ideal neighborhoods, older homes, and so forth. You might choose to get creative at this point—possibly borrow some money from a friend or family member to see if you can afford something a little more expensive. If you are into repairs and home improvement, you might choose to go with something cheaper and fix it up along the way.

If you are buying a house, you will have to think about things like regular maintenance, snow shoveling, grass cutting, and so forth, whereas if you are looking at buying an apartment or a condo, you will pay the homeowner's association (HOA) to do this for you. HOA dues can run anywhere from $150/month to $1,000/month depending on what facilities the condo has. Since you are required to pay the HOA dues every month as an owner, make sure you can afford the mortgage plus the dues.

When I was looking for a condo in Los Angeles, the amount of cash I had and the monthly payment I could afford (while still paying over $2,000/month toward outstanding student loans) limited me to older one- to two-bedroom condos in decent neighborhoods or three- to four-bedroom houses in up-and-coming neighborhoods like South Central Los Angeles and Compton. The fact that I could only afford maybe 10 percent of properties on the market was a great thing, because my search went a lot faster and I could eliminate options quickly.

Step 3: Contact the agents from the listings you like and go on viewings with a few different agents until you find someone you trust and feel comfortable around.

In the beginning, you need to take some time to feel out real estate agents. Some are smart, kind, and trustworthy; others are condescending, sales-y idiots. A good real estate agent can be a long-lasting friend. (I still go out to dinner once a month with my agent.) He or she will be your number-one fan with sellers and will confidently boast how awesome you are and why they should give you the best deal. They will read every clause of every piece of paperwork to make sure you're not getting ripped off and, in some extreme cases, even lower commission with the seller so that you can afford more house. A good real estate agent is a person you can excitedly text at 11:30 p.m. from your bed as you browse Zillow and find something amazing. They will drive all over creation tirelessly with you and bring coolers full of water and Clif bars to make it through long days of viewings. Good real estate agents are *awesome*. You will probably sense when you are talking to one because you'll be able to click and joke around and feel like you're in good hands.

Similarly, you'll also know when you are talking to a bad agent. He or she will come across as pushy, ask dumb questions, make boring conversation, and let you do most of the work. To find a good agent, you should contact a few people at first and have them show you a property—or two or three.

Step 4: Write several offers.

If you are working with a nonconventional loan (which your mortgage broker will inform you on), you may come across homes that don't want to sell to people using nontraditional types of loans. You may also see some places that are slightly out of your range and decide to make lowball offers. All of this is fine. Your real estate agent and mortgage broker will do whatever paperwork is necessary for placing offers on as many properties as you want, and they will do it with a smile. If multiple offers get accepted, it's no problem, because in almost all cases, you'll have up to three days to make your decision and put money down on only one of them. It costs nothing to make offers—nothing to you, your mortgage broker, or your real estate agent.

Step 5: Once one of your offers is accepted, just do what you are told.

After a few weeks of seeing properties and writing offers, finally one will be accepted. This is sort of the beginning of the end. You will now need to work on a ridiculous amount of paperwork and negotiation. Your mortgage broker will request tax returns, paycheck stubs, and statements from any asset or liability you have, such as bank statements, credit card bills, student loan statements, retirement savings, and the like. Your real estate agent will be busy setting up home inspections, which you may need to attend and evaluate. After about a month or two of running around like a crazy person, you'll make your down payment and collect your keys. With a little more work, you can spruce up the place you just bought and feel a huge and overwhelming sense of pride, telling people, "I just bought a little place in [insert city or neighborhood here]."

Every mortgage payment, which will probably be similar to if not slightly higher or lower than your previous rent payment, is money you will probably see again whenever you sell your house. Gone are the days of flushing money down the toilet via rent.

Alternative Ways to Avoid Paying Rent

Now, maybe you fall into a group of people who truly can't make the above suggestions work. If buying property just isn't an option for you, there are other ways to avoid paying rent. Here are a few options.

Become an Expatriate

I had just moved back to the United States after working abroad for the past six years. To some extent, the party was over. When I told other Americans that I had moved to Los Angeles from Singapore, and not Wichita or Des Moines as they were expecting, most looked at me like I was Lindsay Lohan's character from *Mean Girls*. For the first time in my life, I related to Lindsay Lohan (at least, her character in the movie). I was baffled by company health insurance plans. *HMO? PPO? The money comes out of my paycheck?!* I was shocked when I visited the doctor and found out that I still had to pay for prescriptions that were, for some reason, not covered by this expensive insurance policy. I developed major anxiety in the car, frantically reminding myself out loud when making left-hand turns that "they drive on the *right* side of the road, they drive on the right . . ." I almost rethought my decision to move back to the United States. After monthly necessities and loans were paid, I had only a little over $1,000/month in spending money. This is a far cry from the $9,000/month of free cash I had in Singapore. The days of yacht parties and weekend dive trips were over. *We're flying economy now, baby.*

The reason it doesn't bother me now is that for the past few years, I truly did live a life that is pretty unimaginable by most people in six-figure student loan debt. I traveled internationally once a month, stayed in five-star hotels, was in the best shape of my life thanks to my personal trainers, and celebrated friends' birthdays on private islands. People never hear about these sides of expatriate life, usually because those of us experiencing it feel too guilty to brag to friends. My spending money after paying tax and about $3,000 of student debt per month was close to $6,500, largely because I had no rent, no mortgage, no car, and no gas or parking expenses. That may or may not sound like a lot of money to everyone, but it was a lot to me.

How did I do it? Two words: expat package. In Singapore, I met a guy who had come to Singapore with the same company he worked for in the United Kingdom, and as part of his contract, he was given a $3,700 budget for rent, a leased car completely paid for by the company, and reimbursement for all of his gas and parking as well. One of my American friends did digital marketing for a prominent car company there and got a smaller living stipend plus a free car.

Are such deals common? Pessimistic readers will claim "Of course not!" and write off any notion that this could be a potentially useful strategy for paying down debt. They would sort of be right—it's a lot harder to find an expat package than staying where you are, making a modest salary, paying rent, and living on a few hundred dollars after you pay your student loans. Regardless: while not common, neither impossible.

Other Ways to Live for Free

Let's start by discussing the options you probably think I'm talking about but am not. They are the basic advice that comes up when you Google "live for free" and whatnot—articles that suggest you live on a farm or "couch-surf" or whatever. Personally, I would not do any of those things at this juncture of my life (although I did live on a farm for free on a tropical island in Malaysia one summer, and it was pretty cool; that was, however, before I was in payoff mode on my student loans). There's a difference between living for free by barely scraping by and living for free the smart way.

I will run through these options quickly on the off chance you have not heard of them and in case one can work for your situation.

WWOOF (World Wide Opportunities on Organic Farms, wwoof.net)

How it works:

You join the site, look at opportunities in 120 different countries, and then choose based on what you have to do and what your accommodation would be like. In some places, you would be expected to work eight to nine hours a day, five days per week, and live in a barn; at the place I chose, I worked about 3.5 hours a day and lived at a tropical resort on an island, in one of the rooms.

Why it's not a good debt payoff strategy:

You are not paid for your work but given accommodation and food. It is actually a pretty cool way to travel, but I don't see anyone paying off six-figure student debt this way.

Housesitting (www.trustedhousesitters.com/us/, www.housecarers.com, www.mindmyhouse.com, www.housetravels.nl, www.caretaker.org, and more)

How it works:

You join the site and look at opportunities to live in someone's house for free while they travel. You will probably be expected to deal with house maintenance and pets if they have any. You are not paid to work, but you get free housing.

Why it's not a good debt payoff strategy:

I feel it would be too hard to work a demanding job while constantly moving and looking for more opportunities in the same city.

Home exchange or couch-surfing (www.homeexchange.com, www.couchsurfing.com)

How it works:

You join the site, communicate with other members, and stay for free at their homes as you travel through the area.

Why it's not a good student debt payoff strategy:

It could be, if you found someone cool that didn't mind how long you stayed. However, the mentality behind these sites is that people who offer their spaces want to help travelers and meet different people, so I'm not sure how easy it would be to find someone open to long-term, free living situations. Worth a try, I guess?

Potentially Better Ways to Live for Free

Live for free, in exchange for helping take care of someone, usually an elderly or disabled person (nationalsharedhousing.org, or type in the phrase "disabled in home" into other job searching websites)

How it works:

These situations are very nuanced and individualized, so it's hard to completely explain, but the basic scenario is that one joins, finds an arrangement in their area, and gets free or very cheap housing in exchange for some help around the house.

Why it could be a good debt payoff strategy:

The placements are long term, and some that I read about didn't sound that bad. One person got to live with an elderly couple for free on the condition that she drove them to the grocery store twice a week. Another guy got a long-term, free room in exchange for house and pet sitting every time the owner traveled, which was a lot.

The downside:

Not everyone wants to work a job, come home, and work more. I don't. I also don't want to live with people I'm not totally comfortable with.

Work as a live-in nanny or au pair (www.aupair.com, www. aupairworld.com, www.greataupair.com, www.care.com— anything that comes up when you Google "professional household staff placement") or on a cruise ship (www. cruiseshipjob.com/; www.allcruisejobs.com; www.ncl.com/ about/careers/overview; jobs.carnival.com; www.princess. com/careers/)

How it works:

An au pair is a nanny who lives with a (usually extremely wealthy) family in their home and takes care of their kids. Working on a cruise ship means you literally live on a cruise ship and work in entertainment, food and beverage, or customer service.

Why it could be a good debt payoff strategy:

Some of these jobs, particularly the au pair ones, can be quite lucrative. However, you probably need to work at least one less-lucrative job to move up in pay scale. I personally know families who pay their nannies $100–$140K, and the nanny gets to travel with the family, stay in five-star hotels, fly business class, have all their food paid for, and in some cases receive "perks" like designer bags, sunglasses, and Christmas bonuses. You also pay very little tax if you're placed overseas.

The downside:

If you don't want to do these jobs as a career, and taking one means you might lose traction on a career you're working toward, there is no reason to take such a big sidetrack. Not everyone has it in them to take care of kids or tourists.

Property or apartment manager

How it works:

You work as a property manager, living in an apartment complex for free and dealing with tenant move-in, move-out, maintenance issues, lease paperwork, etc.

Why it could be a good debt payoff strategy:

If the money you earn and the rent you don't have to pay puts you in a financially better place than your current situation, it's a win. It would be an even better payoff strategy if you could actually work a normal day job related to your career and somehow pull this job off to get the free housing.

The downside:

The "free" housing could be taxable.

Live with family

How it works:

You move in with your parents or some other generous family member who allows you to stay with them without paying rent.

Why it could be a good debt payoff strategy:

As long as you have viable work options in whatever area they live in, you don't have to change much else about your lifestyle.

The downside:

Sometimes living with family can be challenging, especially if you're used to your independence.

Other ideas: live in an RV; have your roommates pay your rent

Yeah, you could buy an RV and park it in your friend's driveway. However, if you have enough spare cash for an RV, you might as well use it for a down payment on a house, since a house is more likely to be an appreciating asset, whereas a vehicle is more likely to lose value over time.

If you are lucky enough to have or find an apartment with multiple rooms, you could attempt to live in the basement or a small bedroom and then rent out the "good" rooms for the total price of the rent. I did this once in San Francisco. I found a Victorian house that was listed as a two-bedroom, but upon visiting, I discovered it had additional rooms with doors that served as the living and dining room and a tiny space called "the box room." Total rent on the house was around $3150 (this was in 2005). I rented the box room, large bedroom, and giant living/dining room out for $500, $800, and $1350, thereby reducing my own rent on a decent-sized bedroom to $500. The only way this works is if you can find an odd-ish space that can be divided into multiple rooms and roommates willing to pay—presuming you aren't breaking any zoning laws or owner/building restrictions.

If none of these opportunities sound like you, it's time to sophisticate your job search. Just look for jobs with free housing. There are some in the United States and some abroad. Search for job sites with paid housing. Go to Google and enter "paid housing jobs." Indeed should rank them by state. In Monster, type in "free housing." Some jobs I found that offer free housing are:

- Nursing
- Property manager
- Physical therapist
- Psychologist
- Nature programs
- Manufacturing
- Botanist
- Accounts payable
- Residence coordinator
- Digital marketing
- Social worker

Ways to Live for Cheap

If you can't live for free, why not live for cheap? Here are some US cities and states that offer perks just for living there.

Washington (www.wsac.wa.gov/health-professionals)

Washington's Health Professional programs offer up to $75,000 in student loan repayment for doctors, nurses, pharmacists, and others working in rural or underserved areas.

New Haven, Connecticut (renewhavenct.com)

Receive up to $10,000 to buy a home in New Haven, Connecticut, to use as a down payment or for closing costs. If you live in the house for five years, the loan is 100 percent forgivable. You receive an additional $2500 if you're a city employee, teacher, police officer, firefighter, or member of the military. Additionally, they offer $30,000 for energy-saving home upgrades (in the form of a forgivable loan after ten years).

Baltimore, Maryland

The Buying Into Baltimore Program (livebaltimore.com/financial-incentives/details/buying-into-baltimore/) offers first-time homebuyers $5,000 toward buying anywhere in the city.

The Live Near Your Work Program (livebaltimore.com/live-near-your-work/), also for first-time homebuyers, is a $2,000–$5,000 grant or conditional grant (half from City of Baltimore and half from an employer) to be used toward down payment and closing assistance. City employees can receive up to $5,000 toward buying a home.

If moving into an abandoned home and renovating it appeals to you, the city's Vacants to Value Program (www.vacantstovalue.org/) will give you $10,000 in down payment and closing cost assistance. The program also offers the grant to eligible buyers of previously vacant homes that have been rehabbed.

Marquette, Kansas (www.freelandks.com)

If building and land is more of your thing, consider Marquette. They will give a free plot of land to anyone who successfully builds a home on it within one year. The city will waive all building permit fees and utility hook-up fees.

Lincoln, Kansas (www.lincolnks.org)

Kansas has two other incentives for living there. The first is a building incentive similar to Marquette, in Lincoln (www.lincolnks.org). If you can build, you can have free land.

Their other incentive, called Rural Opportunity Zones, offers no state income tax for five years and student loan repayment of up to $15,000 over five years to out-of-state taxpayers who relocate to and establish a home in any of the designated seventy-seven counties. Obviously, the catch is that you would have to find a decent-paying job that would allow you to pay more than you can now, as the income tax and student loan reductions are pretty small. For more details, visit kansascommerce.gov/320/Rural-Opportunity-Zones.

Curtis, Nebraska (www.curtis-ne.com/freelots.php); New Richland, Minnesota (www.cityofnewrichlandmn.com/?SEC=E4182CA2-FBE7-4271-89BD-2907B9067956); or Harmony, Minnesota (www.harmony.mn.us)

Curtis and New Richland have their own variations of the "free land" deal, similar to the ones offered in Marquette and Lincoln, and in Harmony, you get a rebate of $5,000–$12,000 once your new home is finished.

Maine (maineventurefund.com/)

Aspiring entrepreneurs should consider Maine. The Maine Venture Fund is a professionally managed venture capital fund that invests exclusively in Maine companies that demonstrate a potential for significant growth and/or public benefit. By simply living in Maine, you can potentially get free funding from the state for your new business.

Alaska

This benefit is almost too tiny to mention, but if you have residency in the state of Alaska, you are entitled to an annual check for the oil in Alaska through the Permanent Fund Dividend Division. The payout averages about $1200 per year but can vary. For more details, visit http://pfd.alaska.gov.

Have I convinced you to stop paying rent? This list has probably been exhausting to read, and maybe you still feel like none of the options are feasible for you. That's OK! The point is that you are starting to think in new directions—in terms of options instead of limitations. No book or person ever made me do anything differently before I was ready. Sometimes information is like a seed in your brain that you don't realize is there until it sprouts up later. A good starting point is to simply remember that you have choices. These aren't the easiest suggestions to execute, but if you can, you might eventually open yourself up to a life of new possibilities that take you a lot further than canceling your Netflix subscription would.

Notes

1. Vasel, K. (2016, June 22). 11 million Americans spend half their income on rent. CNN Money. Retrieved February 12, 2017, from money.cnn.com/2016/06/22/real_estate/rent-affordability-housing-harvard/index.html.

CHAPTER 5

YOUR NEW SIX-FIGURE JOB

T here are so many things about our current education system and most career paths that have always been confusing to me. Some are:

- Why does it seem like high-paying fields (such as medicine and law) require expensive schooling that forces students to graduate with crippling debt, and yet there is no guarantee that they'll make enough money in their jobs to pay it off?
- Why do so many jobs attempt to "start you at the bottom" but don't really have any guarantee of gradual upward momentum?
- Why does it seem impossible to change industries or job focus without completely starting at the bottom again, even if you have a higher-ed degree?
- Why does it sometimes appear that higher education degrees presume to give one a "leg up" in their career or chosen field

yet, after getting one, it seems that work experience would have been more helpful?
- Why are some industries so hard to break into?
- What career paths lead to high-paying jobs these days?
- Is it really worth "doing what you love" if you can never make any money at it?

Maybe these sound like pessimistic questions, and I guess to some extent they are. But they are questions I really had and sometimes still do have. I felt like some people got the manual for life and I didn't. We've become so adept at marketing how "amazing" our lives are on social media platforms that it's hard to know how happy anyone is, how financially successful they are, whether they've actually been promoted at work, or if they feel their degree was worth getting.

I remember being very fixated on whether I was "using" my degree. I felt like a failure when I wasn't, because it made the ridiculous amount of debt I was in seem so stupid. What kind of person would sink a portion of their salary for the next twenty to twenty-five years into a career they either couldn't obtain or no longer wanted? My answer was "A very dumb one"—in other words, me.

In this chapter, I will attempt to answer some of the questions asked above. I assume you might be asking them too.

Part 1: Degrees and study programs worth the investment

In the financial world, we often talk about ROI, or "return on investment." ROI is used to evaluate whether to put money into a particular investment, property, or business endeavor. It is the tool of any smart person looking to put their money somewhere. Back in the '80s and '90s, when the economy was booming, it made sense to say "study what you love" or "figure out what you love doing." Feelings were a big factor in choosing a career. But we are not in the '80s and '90s anymore. You no longer own parachute pants or scrunchies, listen to MC Hammer, or wear overalls with only one buckle clipped. Different rules apply.

Different rules should apply to thought processes around careers and educational investments as well, yet for most of us, they don't.

Many of us are paying the price for this now. Of course, some of you maybe knew this intrinsically or were pushed by your parents to get a "stable" degree like engineering, business, or finance. I am going to assume that not all of us are in that boat. Before we talk about the degrees and careers with the biggest ROI, let's look at the ones with the lowest.

Salary.com recently did a survey of the careers with the worst return on investment.[1] To calculate ROI for a specific degree, they assumed a four-year degree cost of $37,343 for a public liberal arts degree and $121,930 for degrees earned at four-year private colleges. The total included room and board, tuition, and books; it did not include scholarships or grants. They then determined the median cash compensation over the course of thirty years of typical jobs requiring that degree, adding 4.3 percent per year to account for inflation. To determine ROI, they subtracted the cost of the degree from the gains over thirty years and divided that figure by cost.

The careers and degrees with the worst return on investment are:

1. Sociology (working as a social worker, corrections officer, or chemical dependency counselor)
2. Fine arts (working as a museum researcher, graphic designer, painter, or illustrator)
3. Education (working as a daycare teacher, elementary school teacher, or high school teacher)
4. Religious studies/theology (working as a chaplain in the health care sector, associate pastor, or religious educator)
5. Hospitality/tourism (working as a meeting or event planner, hotel resident manager, or catering manager)
6. Nutrition (working as a dietician, food services manager, or food scientist)
7. Psychology (working as a human services worker, career counselor, or bereavement coordinator)
8. Communications (working as a copywriter, news reporter, or marketing coordinator)

Did you just read through that list and think, *Dang—all the things I thought about doing as a career!* (Maybe that was just me.)

If you are already through undergraduate education, you may be more interested in the graduate degrees with best and worst returns on investment. In 2016, *Fortune* magazine did an article on the graduate degrees with best and worst ROI. They ran numbers with PayScale analysts, considering factors such as long-term outlook for job growth (according to the Bureau of Labor Statistics' Employment Projections data from 2014 to 2024), median pay at ten or more years of experience, and job satisfaction rates.[2]

The top fifteen were:

1. master's, biostatistics
2. master's, statistics
3. PhD, computer science[3]
4. PhD, economics
5. master's, applied mathematics
6. master's, computer science
7. PhD, pharmacy
8. PhD, mathematics
9. PhD, physics
10. master's, software engineering
11. PhD, physical chemistry
12. master's, information systems
13. master's, physician assistant studies
14. MBA, management information systems
15. PhD, political science

The highest median salaries from the above list (i.e., having ten or more years of experience) were $147,400 (PhD, computer science) and $137,800 (PhD, physics), and the lowest median salary was $103,600 (master's in physician assistant studies).

The worst fifteen graduate degrees were:

1. master of fine arts (MFA)
2. master's, early childhood education
3. master of divinity (MDiv)—tied with master's in elementary education

4. master's, elementary education—tied with master of divinity
5. master's, reading and literacy
6. master's, theology
7. master's, special education
8. master's, graphic design
9. master of library and information science (MLIS)
10. master of arts in teaching (MAT)
11. master's, curriculum and instruction
12. master's, teaching English as a second language (ESL or TESOL)—tied with master's in pastoral ministry
13. master's, pastoral ministry—tied with master's in ESL/ TESOL
14. master of architecture (MArch)
15. master's, English literature

The highest median salary from the above list was $81,100 (master's in architecture), and the lowest median salary from the above list was $46,600 (master's in fine arts). Guess what my degree is? You guessed it: a master of fine arts. Awesome.

An issue I had when I would research high-paying careers is that I couldn't seem to find anything that more or less "guaranteed" pay of $140K or more in the first few years. We have a very large country; a lot of salary medians and averages get skewed by the sheer number of people doing jobs for low pay, and it is very difficult to get data from every single person doing any particular career.

Here's another thing that never made sense to me: when I left Silicon Valley as a technical recruiter to go to graduate school, I was making about $62K/year. When I got out of grad school with a mater's degree (albeit in film), entry-level jobs I was hoping to get as the result of my unpaid internship paid between $30K and $45K. Why? Because I didn't have any experience. Aside from the fact that this made my expensive graduate school investment seem even more silly, it also made it almost impossible for me to actually *work* in the field I'd gone to graduate school for given the amount of student loan debt I had.

Part 2: How to get a job with little to no experience

Why is starting or changing a career synonymous with fear, stress, and financial instability? It doesn't have to be.

Most of us come from a generation where school was supposed to give us a leg up over non–degree holders. Nowadays, many graduate degree holders find themselves entering the workforce with the exact same opportunities as everyone else. Here's how can you overcome the odds (along with your own self-doubt).

First off, assume you are just as smart, competent, and qualified as everyone else. Having a lot of debt does not make you a stupid person. Being lazy at work and not taking advantage of opportunities to their fullest, however, is stupid. We need to throw out the idea that a paycheck validates one's ability to be good at a job. Being paid to do something doesn't determine whether you *are* that "thing." Is a salesperson a salesperson because they work in sales—or is it because they can get you to cancel your existing dinner reservation in favor of a place they are just *convinced* you will enjoy more?

If you are thinking of making a career change—either because you want to get into an industry you will earn more in or enjoy more *or* because you finished graduate school recently and are light on actual paid experience—here are some ways you can set yourself up for success in this transition.

1. Determine the absolute lowest amount of money you need to live on without going overboard.

Be completely honest, and be generous with your figures. Do not make promises that in order to keep will result in an uncomfortable, joy-free existence. Never say things like "I'll never drink Starbucks again" or "I will stop going out" or "I'll cancel my gym membership." Going to the gym is healthy and keeps us sane. Starbucks typically does too. And you need to see your friends and connect with other human beings.

If your student loans are $1,500 per month, take this into account. Make a promise to yourself not to accept anything less than what you honestly need to get by, then convert this into an annual salary. Do not judge the number, thinking, *Experienced people can't even demand that salary; there's no way I'll be able to.* We will deal with that later.

2. Find three jobs you want and/or companies you want to work for.

Instead of spending hours blasting out résumés that you spent even more time hand-tailoring to each job post, save yourself the time and energy and get smarter about attacking your job search. When you are trying to get into a new field, the *weakest* part of your application is your résumé. Either you have the years of experience or you don't. If you don't, HR will be uncomfortable going to bat for you. They are also trying to look competent.

Obviously, you need to remain realistic. You cannot market yourself as a brain surgeon if you didn't go to medical school or a lawyer if you didn't pass the bar. Most other jobs are fair game. If the position you're interested in appears to have been posted by a recruiter and you cannot find the actual company with a simple Google search, find another opportunity more worthy of your time and application. I learned during my brief stint with technical recruiting that recruiters are typically paid to find the most obvious, targeted version of what the client thinks they want, not leaving much room for a more "unconventional" candidate with potential.

3. Once you've chosen three opportunities, make two lists of skills or experiences from the job postings: skills that you HAVE and skills that you DON'T HAVE.

Look over the requirements listed on the jobs and see where you fall short. Let's say I am interested in entering the field of security. I currently have an arts degree (stop laughing—I can hear you). Upon researching,

I find a job posting for a position called "Intelligence Analyst Sr" for the US Postal Service. I read the "Desirable Qualifications" section first. They are looking for:

- A bachelor's or master's degree in statistics, computer science, digital forensics, engineering, IT, or finance. | ✘ *DO NOT HAVE*
- Experience with link analysis in utilizing IBM i2 Analyst's Notebook, Microsoft Visio, or an equivalent visualization platform. | ❓ *I CAN PROBABLY FIGURE THIS OUT*
- The ability to apply analysis using software tools such as MS Excel. | ✔ *I CAN DEFINITELY DO THIS*
- Experience in providing presentations to various levels of leadership and audiences. | ✔ *SURE*

I go on to read the duties and responsibilities of the job. It sounds like the role involves collaborating with field managers in the collection, evaluation, and reporting of intelligence data, providing direction to field units on data collection, and monitoring investigative analyst programs. There is more, but these are the main takeaways.

So what does my actual work experience look like?

- Executive assistant at a hedge fund
- Film production management
- Teaching assistant at a university

The next thing we are going to do is spin my existing experience and make me an ideal candidate for this role. Let's revisit the job requirements:

1. A bachelor's or master's degree in statistics, computer science, digital forensics, engineering, IT, or finance.

First of all, recognize that this specific list of degrees basically translates to: "We want a smart person who knows math." Most degrees require classwork in some kind of math. I have bachelor's degrees in international business and psychology. I studied statistics for both majors, and a lot of my business classes involved quantitative analysis. I might say I have a bachelor of science and leave it at that (preparing to walk them through my math experience in the interview), or I might change "Major" to "Focus" or "Areas of Study" so I can specifically list statistics and quantitative analysis.

2. Experience with link analysis in utilizing IBM i2 Analyst's Notebook, Microsoft Visio, or an equivalent visualization platform.

I have no idea what any of these things are. I go to Udemy, a popular website for free or cheap online courses, and search "data visualization." I find a course for $10.99, created by the Analytics Training Institute, that takes two hours and seventeen minutes to complete. It comes with a certificate of completion.[4]

I read the reviews; people mention coming out of the course with charts they can use for their portfolios. Great! I sign up.

3. Experience with MS Excel; 4. Providing presentations to leadership.

After I watch the Udemy video and create my charts, I take note of my Excel, management, and presentation skills—all things I have experience with. After reviewing examples of good cover letters online, I draft mine and update my résumé to ensure both documents highlight these experiences.

Five days later, I send the US Postal Service a polished résumé with a glowing cover letter that reassures the reader of my competence, leadership abilities, and presentation skills along with the charts I made with the Udemy video, which I refer to as a "data visualization portfolio." I send these items to both the email address listing on the job posting and the Director of Intelligence, whose name I find on LinkedIn. Why can you feel confident that this approach will very likely result in an interview? First off, the number of people who send portfolios to noncreative jobs without being prompted to in the job posting is likely pretty small. Second, the job's annual salary is listed as $60–100K. A $100K job may sound like a lot of money, but it's not— especially for fields like statistics and big data. Trust me, the really experienced person you're worried about getting the job instead of you already works somewhere else for $160K. Really. Third, if you're smart enough to take these steps, you are definitely smart enough for this position. I have no doubt.

In 2015, Money Under 30 reported that 46 percent of Americans in their twenties earned under $25K per year.[5] You can pretty much bet the number does not leap into six figures from age twenty-nine to thirty. Stop believing you have to start at the bottom and work for less than you're worth. Bolster your application process (and how about your confidence while we're at it?) and go for it.

Part 3: Impenetrable industries: how to make yourself stand out

Ever feel like you're barking up the wrong tree, for lack of a better idiom? We've all been there. Plenty of industries have well-earned reputations of being hard to get into—the medical field, journalism, the music industry, professional sports, film and television, art, and fashion (just to name a few).

Did you just read this list and again think, *But those are all the things that interest me!*? You're not alone.

It's easy to overcomplicate the job search process and think your industry is especially challenging to be successful in. This is a self-limiting belief, and it's always easier to engage in a self-limiting belief than to face the fear behind it. Self-limiting beliefs may protect our egos, but they rarely have a positive effect on happiness. I'll share a quick example of someone who did not let a self-limiting belief hold him back and how it paid off for him.

One time I was working at my hedge fund job in Singapore. My boss came in and told me, "Someone wrote to me on LinkedIn from a submarine—make sure I respond."

I was confused and intrigued, so I logged into his LinkedIn and printed the message. It was from a guy who was in the Navy, currently serving as a nuclear surface warfare officer. Apparently, his sub had docked somewhere, and he wrote to my boss (who was a prominent figure in the finance world) saying he was looking for a job. He had held a four-month internship that sort of had something to do with finance six years prior for a government body. The next thing I knew, my boss set up a call for this guy and we arranged for him to meet a partner in our New York office the next time he docked there. Despite not having a finance degree, he ended up getting a job as an analyst with us—a job that typically went to people with much different on-paper qualifications than his. Historically, my boss responded to about one percent of his LinkedIn messages. He could not resist responding to this one because the guy wrote a cool story about his background.

Do you have a "cool story" about your past? I bet you do but don't think it's that cool. Think about what you could spin. Maybe you're thinking, *My industry doesn't work like that.* OK. What does your industry value? Creativity? A portfolio? A PowerPoint presentation about how you could solve a problem at the company you're applying for? Think of *one* way to differentiate yourself; one is all you need when the majority of job applicants passively send résumés.

Looking for more industry-specific ideas? Here are some I came up with:

- Write an article about whatever industry or company you're trying to work for and submit it with your CV. If you're trying to work at an art gallery, do a review of another art show or artist. If you want to break into the music industry, compare and contrast two albums by the same artist. If it's sales, review the company's product against its competitors and talk about the relative pros and cons.
- If you want a job at a film production company, find a film that really flopped recently and do a PowerPoint presentation on a cool social media campaign they could have run.
- Make a small video pitch or introduction and send it with your application or put it on your LinkedIn.
- Have friends write LinkedIn recommendations on your page in exchange for you writing one on theirs.
- If you do, say, amateur photography, create a free online portfolio and put twenty of your best shots on there. You will

look more well rounded.
- Make a Spotify playlist for the manager you're reaching out to (this would likely only be well-received in, say, cool Silicon Valley startups), and explain why you think they would like it.

If you don't have time to do this yourself, hire someone from Upwork to do the grunt work while you direct the workflow. While you're at it, have someone touch up your CV and cover letter as well. Sometimes it's easier to edit someone else's work than start completely from scratch.

Can I *guarantee* that any of these things will work? Of course not. But can I guarantee that it will differentiate you from most of the other candidates? Definitely. Most managers will really respond to what you're doing. Some won't. Some will open your email on the wrong day. That's why you're going to follow this process at least three times for three specific jobs. Only one needs to think you're amazing.

Part 4: The fastest way to a six-figure job

This is a question that used to boggle my mind. Have you ever met a friend, found out what they made, and were completely blown away because you had *no idea* that one could make that much in their job role?

A lot of high-paying jobs are not advertised, or if they are, they don't state the salary because they don't want their inboxes to be flooded with people who have no qualifications but apply "just in case." Other high-paying jobs are primarily filled by recruitment agencies.

This section is going to focus on two things: choosing a job that will lead to a six-figure paycheck and turning a current job into a six-figure job.

New career paths

The following is a comprehensive list of new career paths you could take to quickly get on track for higher future earnings in a few years or less.

Real estate agent

Annual earning potential:

$180,000+.

What you need:

A real estate license and a car.

Time/money investment:

About $1,000 and 2–3 months.

Easiest and cheapest way to get a real estate license:

1. Complete the required pre-licensing courses, which vary by state. They can usually be completed at a community college, either in special night courses or online. States can require anywhere from 60 to 180 hours of these courses.
2. Pass the licensing exam. Depending on the state, the exam can take anywhere from 90 minutes to 4 hours, and you usually need to get 70–75 percent of questions right to pass. You will need to study for the exam and may choose to enroll in another prep course. (Alternatively, check for smartphone study apps.)
3. Submit your license application. Check reciprocity agreements between states. With a California real estate license, you can only work in California, but with a New York license, you can work in nine other states as well.
4. Find a sponsoring broker to associate your license with. Your license is not active until you do so.

Emergency manager

Annual earning potential:

In large cities, $160,000+.

What you need:

Experience and a certified emergency manager license.

Time/money investment:

About $595 and one year.

How to get certified:

1. Go to the International Association of Emergency Managers at iaem.com and find a job. There is a large international job board with many opportunities. Job postings sometimes ask for a degree in emergency management or homeland security, but since emergency management is a relatively new field, most will consider applicants with experience related to writing, planning, project management, archiving, or computer programming.
2. Once you have one year of experience, you can fill out an application to become certified.
3. If your application is accepted, you pay $595 and take a 100-question multiple-choice exam.

Data scientist

Annual earning potential:

$119,000 (entry level) to $250,000+.

What you need:

Experience programming (writing code) or studying or using statistics.

Time/money investment:

Varies. Data Science for Social Good offers a three-month fellowship through the University of Chicago, which is free if you get accepted. Others range in price from $3K to $20K and last about three to four months. For a comprehensive review of 2018 data science bootcamps, visit   www.cio.com/article/3051124/careers-staffing/10-boot-camps-to-kick-start-your-data-science-career.html.

Financial planner

Annual earning potential:

$140,000+.

Time/money investment:

As short as two years and $4,595 on an apprentice track (where you are paid little to nothing during the two years) or as long as 3.5–4.5 years while you complete a CFP Board–registered education program (where you can keep your regular job and study on the side).

How to get certified:

1. Visit the Center for Financial Planning website at www.cfp. net.
2. Under the "Become a CFP Professional" tab, navigate down to "Find a Program" and search by state or certification type. Enroll in a CFP Board–registered Certification Exam course, choosing either an in-person or online program. (If you are a licensed attorney, CFA, ChFC, or CLU or hold a PhD in business or economics, you don't need to do the CFP Examination course.)
3. While you are completing your course, start working or interning. You need either two years as an apprentice to a CFP professional or three years of experience doing personal financial planning, gathering data, analyzing clients' finances, making recommendations, implementing recommendations, teaching, or being in an internship or residency program.
4. When the education and experience criteria have been met, submit your application for approval. Once approved, you can start work as a certified financial planner.

Elevator mechanic

Earning potential:

About 90 percent of people make around $80,000; 10 percent make over $100,000.

Time/money investment:

Five fully paid years, no investment required. The industry is apprenticeship-only.

Process

Search the phrase "elevator apprentice" on job-finding websites such as Indeed and Zip Recruiter, or contact the National Elevator Industry Educational Program (NEIEPP). Further info may be found on www. neiep.org.

Other perks:

Union job (sixty-six unions across the United States); growth is estimated at 25 percent until 2022.[6]

Longshoreman

Earning potential:

Half of West Coast union longshoremen make $100,000; over half of foremen and managers make more than $200,000. A few bosses make over $300,000.[7]

Time/money investment:

$126 for a Transportation Worker Identification Credential (TWIC), which is required for the job, and up to five years of casual work before joining the union. This is not an easy industry to break into, but it can be very lucrative once you get in the union.

Process:

1. Get your TWIC card (a simple application involving a background check—almost as easy as a driver's license).
2. Go to the website of the International Longshore and Warehouse Union if you're on the West Coast (www.ilwu. org) and the International Longshoreman's Association if you're on the East Coast (ilaunion.org).
3. Contact a local union and find out when the hours of the hiring hall are. You start as a "casual worker" and are picked last when work is being assigned. Work hours are early and pay is erratic.
4. Gain enough experience to achieve "identified casual" status.
5. Apply for a union membership. Once you have union membership, you will get regular work and benefits.

Executive personal assistant

Earning potential:

Up to $200,000.

Time/money investment:

In my first year as a hedge fund EA, I started on a base salary of $74,000 and got a $45,000 bonus in my fifteenth month. I easily worked sixty to sixty-five hours per week and dealt with a pretty high amount of stress. If you can get into banking and finance, EA/PA jobs are good—they can definitely reach close to six figures in the first two years.

Other ideas

Here are a few more ideas for careers that can easily become six-figure jobs with limited experience:

- Public relations (PR) specialist
- Social media strategist
- Commercial pilot
- Property manager
- User experience (UX) administrator or designer
- Sales rep
- Marketing manager
- Human resources (HR) manager
- Purchasing manager
- Funeral services manager
- Administrative service manager

Turning your current job into a six-figure job

A lot of jobs can easily produce six-figure salaries with a little know-how. Factors that tie into how fast you can accelerate your earning potential are industry, location, and an honest assessment of your current job.

Industry

With regards to industry, you need to acknowledge that the same job in different industries can pay dramatically different salaries. As a general rule, low-paying industries include government, nonprofit, food and beverage, education, and most creative fields. Industries usually associated with higher pay are technology, science, finance and banking, shipping, energy, oil and gas, and sales (but only if you're good at sales). This point cannot be understated. Way too many smart people work in low-paying industries. A half-decent assistant or coordinator in the Los Angeles film industry starts at $30–$55K/year. The same exact job at a hedge fund can pay $125K/year. Figuring this out was a huge lightbulb moment for me.

Why is it so important to use your skills in whatever industry pays the most for them? Two reasons:

1. It is much easier to go from a high-paying industry to a low-paying one than vice versa.
2. Once you earn a certain salary, you never need to go backward. Start as high as possible to give yourself a head start toward debt-free living.

I was in the middle of a job search recently. I was working in finance, where we usually earn a lower base and a hefty bonus. My current base was $97K, but my last bonus had been $70K. I had a recruiter pitch me a job with a $150K base. I agreed to go for a first-round interview, which went really well. However, when I was asked to go for a second-round interview, I realized that I wouldn't be happy working for $150K when I had made $167K the year before. Even though the base was 50 percent more than what I had been making, the move didn't make sense from a total compensation perspective. I told the recruiter that I couldn't really consider the job unless they could raise the base to $180K–$200K. The point is, when you are already making some money, it's easy to make a little more.

Location

Job location is something that trips people up a lot. Many of us are naturally inclined to live as cheaply as possible when we are in debt. Unfortunately, for some people, that may mean moving back to cheaper cities with family and friends. I personally don't recommend this. Serious salaries are found in serious cities, again with regards to industry. The best cities for jobs in finance and banking are New York, San Francisco, Boston, Dallas, Salt Lake City, Jacksonville, and Chicago.[8] The best cities for jobs in technology are Miami, Detroit, Los Angeles, Phoenix, Charlotte, Dallas, Seattle, San Francisco, and Houston.[9]

Your current job

Let's perform an honest assessment of your current job. Is it the right one for your overall life situation? Are you easily able to pay down your student loan debt and enjoy life in the process? Do you have the financial resources to live like a human being? If not, try to pinpoint what's wrong with your current job. Maybe you're barking up the wrong tree by working in the wrong location or industry. Maybe you're not being aggressive enough in asking for salary increases year by year. Requesting salary increases is necessary because you need to establish whether your current organization is *able* to help you scale your earnings in the way you need.

I was working at a tech company in 2012. I started out as the office manager but quickly took on more and more responsibility that was above and beyond what I was originally hired to do. Six months into the job, I asked for a 75 percent raise. I received only a 50 percent raise. When I saw that my current company was either unwilling or unable to give me what I thought was fair compensation for my work, I instantly started looking for another opportunity that would. I found it in the finance industry, and I went from making $45K in 2012 to $120K in 2014.

If your current job does not offer incentives for taking on more work for more pay, stop waiting and hoping that you will one day be appreciated. Take the initiative to search for new opportunities, always remembering to constantly challenge the limits of what you think your skillsets are worth. If someone is willing to pay $80K, someone else will pay $90K. You are your biggest advocate. Keep pushing, and you may find a six-figure career is more of a possibility than you thought.

Notes

1. Dugan, D. (n.d.). 8 college degrees with the worst return on investment. Salary.com. www.salary.com/articles/8-college-degrees-with-the-worst-return-on-investment/.

2. Dishman, L. (2016, March 21). Best and worst graduate degrees for jobs in 2016. *Fortune*. Retrieved September 30, 2016, from fortune.com/2016/03/21/best-worst-graduate-degrees-jobs-2016/.

3. PayScale's senior editorial director Lydia Frank pointed out that the added cost of a doctorate degree in computer science might not be worth the increase in earning potential because many government-sponsored programs can offer education in programming languages for a fraction of the cost and time via the TechHire initiative.

    (Dishman, Best and worst graduate degrees for jobs in 2016.)

4. You can find it here: www.udemy.com/data-visualization/.

5. Weliver, D. (2015, May 18). "The 2015 Millennial Money Survey: How much do 20-somethings earn and save?" Money Under 30. Retrieved October 14, 2017, from www.moneyunder30.com/20-somethings-money-survey.

6. Anderberg, J. (Updated 2018, October 16). So you want my trade: Elevator mechanic. *The Art of Manliness*. Retrieved October 14, 2017, from www.artofmanliness.com/2015/12/05/so-you-want-my-trade-elevator-mechanic/.

7. Kirkham, C., & Khouri, A. (2015, March 1). How longshoremen command $100K salaries in era of globalization and automation. *Los Angeles Times*. Retrieved October 14, 2017, from www.latimes.com/business/la-fi-dockworker-pay-20150301-story.html#page=1.

8. Butcher, D. (2017, July 12). The top US cities to get a financial services job outside of New York. Retrieved September 16, 2018, from news.efinancialcareers.com/us-en/289772/top-us-cities-to-get-a-financial-services-job-outside-of-new-york.

9. Top US cities for tech hiring. (2018, June 25). Retrieved August 28, 2018, from businessfacilities.com/2018/06/top-u-s-cities-tech-hiring/.

CHAPTER 6

OVERNIGHT CREDIT REPAIR

I n 2011, as I was finishing thesis work in Singapore, I was working as a nanny-slash-personal assistant as well as a teaching assistant in my spare time. I made about $1,300 per month. *It's an interim job,* I told myself, *a job I work until I find something better.*

The first full-time job I received after graduating was an office role, paying $45K/year. It had health insurance, at least. But when I considered the fact that I made $52K/year before grad school working as a recruiter, this felt like another defeat.

My student loans, which would have cost me an impossible $5K/month or so coming right out of school, were deferred for a period after graduation. I applied for an income-based repayment (IBR) plan, under which as long as I paid 10 percent of my income to my student loans (a number much smaller than $5K/month), I did not default. Initially, this sounded great, but what I failed to read between the fine lines was that once I converted each of my different loans from grad school into this singular payment plan, the interest for all of them compounded to the highest interest. *But I should be happy, because at least I only have one payment now . . . correct?*

Another thing *no one* says about income-based repayment is that after twenty-five years, the remaining loan is "forgiven" . . . *but the forgiveness amount will be taxed!*

"Let's look at your loan statement together," my partner urged. It was like he was trying to read my diary. As far as I was concerned, nobody was going to shine a flashlight on this dark corner of my past and get a firsthand glimpse of all the shame and fear that came along with it.

So one day I looked at the statement online, by myself. The first thing I noticed was that I owed almost $286,000 in student loans. Once I got over that shock, I saw my balance was growing at a rate of $1,600/month due to interest.

Income-based repayment is not a break for students. It is a thinly veiled attempt by the government to look like they are giving us a break so they can recoup more money later. Under my IBR plan, I was only required to pay something like $300/month, which I could afford. But before I got too victorious about making these payments, I realized that $300 did not even cover the interest the loan earned *that one month.*

So, in spite of my making payments, my loan balance was increasing by $1,214 every single month.

I thought twenty-five years into the future. If my loan stayed at this rate (not counting inflation) and did not compound, and I kept making the same payments for twenty years, my total would balloon to about $678,000.

Then, when my loan was "forgiven," I would owe the US government tax on $635,000 *as if it were income.* In other words, the government would "forgive" my $635,000 but then act as if I made $635,000 in income that year, and I would owe at least $236,000 on my taxes![1] Did I want to be filing for bankruptcy at the age of fifty-five and going back to living the way I was now?

I distinctly recall feeling like I had been handed a death sentence. Even trying to pay off the debt seemed like a futile effort, as I would not be able to pay it off in any reasonable period of time—and even if I made payments for twenty years, I'd still have to declare bankruptcy. I was thirty years old and had the same amount of debt as people who own a house, but instead of owning a house, I just had a degree—a degree I wasn't even using. Around this time, I thought very seriously about killing myself. I had lost the game. I blamed no one but myself. It felt incredibly pointless to even try paying it off. Who wants to work hard their whole life and, for their efforts, then live in poverty or declare bankruptcy?

No matter how much student debt you have, if you are feeling this way now, I get it. The first thing I had to do was admit I had a problem. This debt was a big problem. I was falling more into debt each month—$1,214 more, in fact. Even if I could have paid $1,600/month at that time (which I couldn't), the payment would, again, *only* cover the interest earned on the loan for that *one* month. None of the principal would be getting reduced, and the next month I'd be at essentially the exact same place as the month before.

This $1,600/month thing really made me angry. It seemed like an unnecessary punishment given the balance of my loan. Why was my interest rate 8.5 percent, anyhow? It was much higher than a mortgage. Does our country value owning a house more than a good education? Sometimes it seems that way.

I fixated on this $1,600/month. I didn't want to pay it. My multimillionaire boss would not have paid it. This is how I discovered student loan refinancing.

Student Loan Refinancing

I kind of sense that your eyes are about to glaze over in boredom, but bear with me. People get confused with the term "student loan refinancing" because we are much more familiar with refinancing homes. When someone refinances their home, it usually means that they are getting a new loan on their property and getting the rest paid out in cash. For example, if a home cost $200,000 and over a few years you've put down $100,000, you can essentially refinance the property and get a check for $100,000 plus a new $200,000 loan.

Student loan refinancing is different. You don't get to pull out any cash, but you can swap your existing loan for a new loan—and preferably one with much lower interest. If your existing student loan is $150,000 with 8.5 percent interest per month and you refinance, you get a new $150,000 loan but the interest might be only 4 percent per month. Essentially, this slows the bleeding hemorrhage of your accumulating interest each month and might mean that your payments actually cover interest *and* principal.

Here are the top student loan refinancing companies according to Consumers Advocate:[2]

- Credible
- Earnest
- Commonbond
- Splash Financial
- SoFi
- LendKey
- Laurel Road
- LendEDU
- LendingTree
- Education Loan Finance

When I was in the midst of my student debt crisis, there were almost no companies doing student loan refinancing. Now it's becoming a competitive industry, which means the interest rates offered could get lower.

Student loan refinancing generally takes two things into consideration: income and credit score. A lot of my former classmates tried to refinance their loans once or twice, got rejected, and are still making those 8.5 percent interest payments. Similarly, I was rejected from every company I tried to refinance with for at least the first year of trying. But whenever my debt balance got a little lower or I started earning more money, I applied again until my application was accepted. (I was *that* annoyed with the $1,600.)

The first time I applied for student debt refinancing, I was $286,000 in debt, was making around $76,000 per year, and had a credit score in the high 600s. Everyone rejected me. It felt awful; the feelings of being a loser and a failure hit me hard. But this time, I shook it off. My strategy and mantra became, "Earn more. Fix credit. Try again." Notice how no refinancing companies care about how much you *spend* per month. This backs my earlier conviction that outgoing cash flow is the wrong place to focus. Income and credit should be your sole focus if you have not yet refinanced your student loans.

People often say that they don't want to refinance their loans because they feel they:

1. Won't be able to write off student loan interest paid on their taxes.
2. Won't be able to forgive their loans in twenty to twenty-five years.
3. Won't be able to cancel the loans if the school they studied at shuts down or is convicted of fraud.

Only the last two are true. While it is true that your loans technically become private loans when you refinance, you still can write off up to $2500 in student loan interest paid on your taxes as long as the lender issues a 1098-E form at the end of the year (which they will, if you're using any of the sites I mentioned above). And while you won't be able to do any loan forgiveness, the fact that the forgiven amount is taxable should have already made you see this option for what it is: a scam (or, if you're less conspiratorial, just a really bad idea). If you are fairly certain your school won't be closed or convicted of fraud any time soon, you can go ahead and refinance.

Maybe you have bad credit and a very low income. I am suggesting you fix both. Let's start with your credit.

Balance Transfer Credit Cards

I will start out by explaining a few things about credit that many people with credit don't know. First, "credit" as it exists on your credit report is a score that reflects your ability to acquire and pay off debt. Good credit means you always pay your debts and bills in full and on time. Bad credit means you don't. Some people think that making lower payments on their credit card bill instead of paying the whole thing off every month is good for their credit score. It's not! Your credit score has nothing to do with how much debt you have; it's based on how you can both acquire and then pay off debt. Similarly, you could be a million dollars in debt but have perfect credit so long as you are paying what you owe on that debt in full each month.

Next—it's pretty unnecessary to have credit card debt earning high interest even if your credit score is low. I'm going to explain how to deal with your credit card debt now so we can move on to student loans. Basically, if you have credit card bills that you can't pay off in full for several months, just get *another* card and do a balance transfer.

A balance transfer is when you move credit card debt onto a new credit card. The new credit card company will offer you a zero percent interest rate for a fixed period of time (usually 12–18 months) and then a high interest rate after. They hope that you will transfer your debt, forget about it, and pay nothing because it's not earning interest—then they will collect your interest money once the zero percent interest period runs out.

You take advantage of their assumptions by getting the balance transfer card and paying it off before any interest is due. This stops the money hemorrhage that high interest is.

The best balance transfer cards as of 2019 are:[3]

Citibank's Simplicity ® Card

- **Pros:** You have 21 months to pay off your debt and no annual fee. This is the longest balance transfer payback period on the market that I'm aware of.
- **Cons:** There's an initial 5 percent balance transfer fee (so if you're transferring $1000 of debt, you will pay $50 as a transfer fee).
- **Your credit score should be:** Approximately 700s or higher

Discover It ® Balance Transfer

- **Pros:** Pay no interest on balance transfers for the first 18 months, and pay no interest on new purchases for the first six months. In addition, whenever you use the card for new purchases, you get between 1–5% cash back. No annual fee.
- **Cons:** There's an initial 4 percent balance transfer fee (so if you're transferring $1000 of debt, you will pay $40 as a transfer fee).
- **Your credit score should be:** Approximately 670s or higher

Discover It ® Secured

- **Pros:** Lower credit scores accepted, 1–2% cash back on new purchases, no annual fee.
- **Cons:** There's no 0% balance transfer period; you can get an introductory interest rate of 10.99% for six months on balance transfers then 25.24% after. If you have a lower credit score, this could still be a lot less than whatever interest you're paying on your credit card currently, and worth some consideration.
- **Your credit score should be:** Approximately 580s or higher

If you have poor credit (a score below 580), you are probably better off getting a debt consolidation loan than a balance transfer credit card. Check out Avant (www.avant.com) or Upgrade (www.upgrade.com), who specifically cater to applicants with bad credit or not much credit history.[4]

Once you get your credit card debt into a manageable place with a manageable interest rate and enough time to pay it off, you can move on to focus on other debts, like student loans!

Fixing Your Credit

When I decided to face my student loans head on so I could stop paying $1600/month in interest, I went on Upwork and found a retired lawyer in New York. For $400, he helped me fix my credit. I will save you this $400 now and give you everything I learned for free.

First, let's summarize the steps we will be walking through on the pathway to credit repair:

1. Find out how bad your credit actually is.
2. Go after the source of the information, which is the three credit reporting agencies (Experian, Equifax, and TransUnion), and try to get them to remove the negative items on your report.
3. If that doesn't work, write to the credit cards, companies, and/or collection agencies to see if they will remove the items—either out of goodwill or as part of a negotiation for you paying or settling the debt.

I will now take you through each step in detail.

Step 1: Find out how bad your credit actually is

You probably think I'm going to recommend you go to FreeCreditReport.com or Credit Karma here. I'm not. In order to really understand what's on your credit, you *must* get scores AND reports from all three credit reporting bureaus: Experian, Equifax, and TransUnion. Whenever you apply for a student loan refinance, mortgage, or credit card, the bank will use one of these methods to check your credit I have seen many occasions where old accounts or negative items show up in one report but not another. Since you don't know if the bank will look at your credit via Experian, Equifax, or TransUnion when evaluating your application, you must know what's on *all three*. Go to www.myfico.com (or a similar site) and pay $29.95 for a monthly membership, which you will immediately cancel right after you get your three reports.

There are many websites and organizations offering "free" credit scores and/or credit reports. In reality, they are usually offering EITHER the score OR the credit report (not both) or scores and reports from only one or two of the three credit reporting agencies (e.g., TransUnion and Experian but not Equifax). You are welcome to go to a bunch of different free services online and try to get each of the reports and scores from each of the three agencies, but I personally think your time taken by visiting multiple websites and create logins and accounts at each site is worth more than $29.95. Not to mention the additional time you'll have to spend deleting all the spam emails you start getting as a result of exchanging your information for something "free."

Print out your three reports and look at them with a highlighter ready. You will see three types of categories on each report: Revolving, Installment, and Open. (In addition, you will likely see any credit cards that you have closed, paid off, or canceled in the past seven years. Keep in mind that a credit report only goes back seven years.) "Revolving" is typically for credit cards, "Installment" consists of mortgages and student loans, and "Open" usually means phone bills and utilities. Highlight any items that show up as late or outstanding. They will likely be printed in red on the report.

This process can be illuminating, enlightening, or downright depressing. I once saw I had a $50 bill on part of an ambulance ride not covered by my insurance. It had been sent to collections after I moved apartments six years earlier and grown to $900. It was seriously hurting my credit, and I was totally unaware of it. Stop living in the dark. Get out your ten bucks and let's start digging.

Step 2: Write to all the reporting agencies (Equifax, Experian, and/or TransUnion) that are showing bad items

We are going to launch a two-pronged attack: first against the reporting agencies themselves and then against the actual places you owe (or supposedly owe) money to. Repeat after me: *all of the bad items on your credit will be disputed.* We are going to think like lawyers here: it's not what you actually paid or didn't pay—it's what the reporting agencies and credit card companies can *prove* you didn't pay. They couldn't care less whether you have something bad on your credit report. You, on the other hand, are paying $1,600/month in interest as a result. Thus, you owe it to yourself to force these places to *prove* that bad item deserves to be on your credit report.

First, look at your credit reports and see if there is any false information—and I mean *any*. This does not only refer to whether you paid the charge in question; it could be any of these things, as well:

- Wrong account number
- Name misspellings
- Inaccurate balance
- Wrong date opened
- Inaccurate account status (e.g., "Closed")
- Inaccurate payment status (e.g., "In collections")
- Incorrect credit limit
- Account is not yours (identity fraud)
- Card was stolen and you can prove you contacted the card company
- Payments missing that you know you made (if you can show a bank statement with the money leaving your account, this is probably the fastest and easiest way to get bad items taken off)

Maybe you were the victim of identity theft. Maybe you had your credit card stolen and you told the credit card company but they never removed the charge. Information that does not appear on all three reports should also be disputed. In any case, your goal here is to find something false about the entry.

Now you're going to write a letter and have it notarized. I don't know why the notarization is necessary, but my lawyer recommended I do it, and I think it is helpful for demonstrating that you stand by your word and have gone the extra step to show it.

Make a list of the errors you find and note what the correct information is. You are going to have to specify a legitimate reason why you think the item is inaccurate.

Sample letter for credit reporting agencies

Next, draft the following letter in typed form:

[Your name]
[Your address]
[City], [State], [zip]
[Your phone number]
[Your social security number]
[Your date of birth]

[Credit reporting agency (e.g., Experian)]
Disputes Department
[Credit reporting agency address]
[City], [State], [zip]

[Date you are writing letter]

To Whom It May Concern at [credit reporting agency you're writing to]:

I recently obtained a copy of my credit report and am writing to dispute some items on it. I have highlighted and numbered these disputed items on an attached copy of the report and will cross-reference the inaccuracies below:

Item 1:
- Credit Agency (e.g., Capital One)
- Reason for Dispute (e.g., Name is misspelled)

Item 2
- Discover
- Payment was made on [date]; see enclosed bank statement.

According to the Fair Credit Reporting Act, your company is required by federal law to verify any and all accounts you request to be posted and/or reported on a credit report.

According to the provisions of the Fair Credit Reporting Act, Section 611, these disputed items must be reinvestigated or deleted from my credit record within 30 days. During the investigation period, these items must be removed from my credit report, as the mere reporting of items prior to debt validation constitutes collection activity. I am also requesting the names, addresses, and telephone numbers of individuals you contacted during your investigation.

Thank you,

[Your name]

With your undeserved bad credit items clearly mapped out and your letters typed, we now need to send them out.

I recommend going to the post office and sending them via certified mail, but in some cases, you can use the company's online portals:

- www.experian.com/disputes
- dispute.transunion.com
- www.equifax.com/personal/disputes

At first glance, it appears that the reporting bureaus make it easy for you to dispute their versions of the truth. Don't be fooled! These websites are generally infuriating and unreliable, and they often ask for information that it appears you should have but is located nowhere. A site may say "Enter your credit report number"—but there is no credit report number listed anywhere on the report! Upon further investigation, you discover that you can only receive a credit report number on a snail-mailed credit report—a request which takes sixty days to process. Be prepared for a lot of frustration; this is only to weed out the less-motivated credit disputers, which, let me assure you, you aren't.

You may want to forgo the online portal altogether for one other reason: many online dispute forms contain arbitration clauses that can undercut your consumer rights. By clicking "I accept" prior to sending the dispute, you may be waiving your rights to sue them if they do something wrong.

Reporting agencies typically offer a mail-in dispute option; if you opt for this route, make sure you take your three letters to the post office so that you can select a tracking or registered mail option. You need proof that these places received your letter.

Notice I just said *three* letters. You will be making three letters because there are three companies (Equifax, Experian, and TransUnion), each holding a report on you.

Please keep in mind: this whole process is not fun. It is worse than going to the gym. Results will take time and effort—even more so if you're anything like me and have never saved a single receipt or credit card statement the past seven years. You may have to request old bank statements and visit post offices and notary publics—it's all a huge pain. The thing to remember about the process is that the potential payoff for success is huge. In addition to the obvious benefit of getting to refinance your student loans and thereby stop the financial hemorrhaging of interest being charged to your account every month, there's an added psychological benefit that is, in my opinion, possibly even more important.

Good credit pays dividends to your financial self-esteem. It means being able to look bankers in the face. It means going shopping for houses and knowing that a mortgage company will give you the one hundred, two hundred, or even five hundred thousand dollars it costs to buy your property. It means feeling like a responsible adult.

Rejection hurts. It hurts when a company says you are not an important enough or trustworthy enough person for them to give money to. It compounds the feelings of failure and depression that your high student debt overhead creates. Think about how it would feel for someone to try to *sell* you a house or car—instead of you begging for one—because you know that your credit is going to check out just fine and make you look good. It's pretty empowering.

I remember when I moved back to the United States and was leasing a car. Seeing that I was unmarried and thirty-four years old, many places asked me if I was *sure* that my credit would check out. Because I had taken all of the actions that I am outlining in this chapter, I knew it would. Before I moved abroad, I think my credit score was about 560 (considered "bad credit"), and when I returned, it was 790 ("excellent credit"). The guy ran my credit report and was surprised. "Wow, yeah—you were right about your credit. It's excellent."

I told him that it used to be in the 500s.

He commented, "That's really great to hear, because I deal with so many people who think that they will never be able to have good credit due to their financial mistakes."

"It's not true," I told him. "Not true at all."

Think about what it feels like to go from throwing credit card and student loan bills directly in the trash (because it's too stressful to look at them) to getting approved for a $500K mortgage. Given the choice, I'd pick the latter.

I only mention all of this because when you write to the credit reporting agencies, you are only half done. Now you need to contact all the credit card places too. It's a daunting process, but just think of the rewards you will reap with improved credit. Read on.

Step 3: Write to the companies (or collection agencies) you owe money to

This next step is similar in theory to the previous step but different in execution. You should only start it *after* you complete the first step (including the waiting period of thirty days while you wait for the credit reporting agencies to respond to your dispute) and fail to get your bad items removed. You are less like a lawyer in this step and more like a panhandler, at first, that will morph into The Godfather later.

First, we are going to assume that people who work at credit card companies are generally good human beings. We will try to appeal to their sense of goodwill and humanity. Below are some examples of correspondences you can use. If you are a married couple, just change the *I*s to *We*s. Please note that the first three letters *do not* apply for debt that has already been sent to a collection agency. If your debt has already gone into collections, you need to skip ahead to the next section, where we'll discuss a different kind of letter you need to write *first*. You may need to follow up by *additionally* writing to the companies the debt originated from, as detailed in this section. But debts in collection or at collection agencies are more damaging to your credit score than late payments, so start there first.

Sample letters for debt not in collections

Example #1: For something you actually did pay late (either in full or an agreed-upon lesser amount) but was never sent to a collection agency

[Your name]
[Your address]
[City], [State], [zip]

[Month and day, year]

[Company name]
[Department name]
[Address]
[City], [State], [zip]
Regarding: Account no. [XXXXX]

Dear [credit card or bank name],

I am writing to see whether [same credit card or bank] would consider making a goodwill adjustment to the credit reporting bureaus on my [closed or open] account. Specifically, I am asking whether [credit card or bank] would remove the adverse late payment and settlement on this account when reporting to the credit bureaus. I understand this is a rather unusual request—particularly as my account [fell behind upward of 120 days ago and was settled for less than the full amount (adjust this sentence as necessary)].

[Credit card or bank] was extremely helpful in working with me at the time of a job layoff and missed payments. The ease with which I was able to resolve the account helped me to settle the matter quickly and move forward.

If what I'm asking is too much, then any goodwill adjustment to the reporting bureaus would be most appreciated.

Regardless of your decision, please know that I thank you for helping me at a time when it was needed, and I hope to do business with [credit card or bank name] again one day.

Best wishes,

[Your name]

Example #2: For something that appears on one credit report but not others and is not in collections

[Your name]
[Your address]
[City], [State], [zip]

[Month and day, year]

[Company name]
[Department name]
[Address]
[City], [State], [zip]
Regarding: Account no. [XXXXX]

Dear [credit card or bank name],

I recently pulled all three of my credit reports. [Credit card or bank name] appears to have mistakenly reported this account as 30 days late to [credit reporting agency—i.e., Experian, TransUnion, or Equifax]. It does not appear on [other two credit reporting agencies]'s report but only [initial credit reporting agency]'s report.

I disputed the account with [credit reporting agency], but either they closed the dispute without checking or there was some problem on their website. In any event, please correctly report this account to [credit reporting agency]—just as it has been reported to the other credit bureaus.

I know mistakes happen and would simply like this corrected. [Lastly, say something about your generally good experiences with the credit company, such as: "Both of my vehicles were purchased new from Ford and financed through you. I have been very happy with both the cars and the payment process, such that I have even recommended friends to follow in my footsteps."]

Sincerely,

[Your name]

Example #3: For an account that you didn't realize was still open on your report but has bad items on it and is not in collections (this works particularly well for credit cards specific to a particular store):

[Your name]
[Your address]
[City], [State], [zip]

[Month and day, year]

[Company name]
[Department name]
[Address]
[City], [State], [zip]
Regarding: Account no. [XXXXX]

Dear [store],

I recently pulled my credit reports and I discovered this [store] credit card account was still showing as open. I was unaware that I still had this account and no longer possess the card.

I also noticed the account was reported 30 days late in [year]. I do not recall being late on this account, but it is possible, as I had recently [describe some hardship here, (e.g., been laid off, finished graduate school, gotten divorced)] and fell behind on a few other payments at that time.

If the late pay reporting is correct, then I would like to ask whether [store] would consider making a goodwill adjustment to its reporting to the credit bureaus and remove the late

pay reporting from this account. I know I am making a somewhat unusual request, but I ask you to consider my overall
good shopping and payment history with [store] rather than
one late payment. Once resolved, I would like to see about
getting a replacement card issued so that I could use it when
shopping at [store].
  Sincerely,
  [Your name]

Send off your letters via certified mail (or with some other kind
of mail tracking) so you can make sure they were received. If you do
not get a reply, you may need to call and reference the letter, noting
the day you can prove it was delivered. This can be an overall tedious
and frustrating process, as follow-up can be slow and laden with people who don't seem to understand or care what you're trying to do.
Persevere.

Sample letter for debt in collections

OK, now what if your debt has already been sent to a collections
agency? No problem. If you have not already paid the debt, *don't pay it
yet*. We are going to play Let's Make a Deal first. All of your negotiating
power lies in the *promise* of paying them, so don't pay it until you write
to them first.

Most collection agencies don't really care how much debt they
collect. In most cases, they have bought the debt off the credit card
company and whatever they can get back is profit for them. Therefore,
if you're going to pay the debt, you might as well get something in
return for it—specifically, your credit back. In the following letter, you
are going to offer to pay the debt off in exchange for the collections
agency not reporting the collection on your credit report. Lest you
think you are not at their mercy (which you definitely are), keep in
mind they have *no* legal obligation to do this. But also keep in mind
that the people who work at these agencies make their careers on how
much they are able to recoup and collect, not how many people's
credit they ruin. What you are proposing is a win-win scenario for

both you and them: you give them their money and they give you back your good credit.

[Collection agency name]
[Collection agency address]
[Collection agency [City], [State], [zip]

Re: Collection Account for Original Creditor Account #: [your account number, as it appears on your credit report]
Amount: [put the amount they are asking for here]

To Whom It May Concern:

This letter is to inform you that I am disputing the validity of this debt. The account number I referenced above is the one listed on my [Experian/TransUnion/Equifax] credit report.

In the spirit of compromise, I am willing to pay this account [either "in full" or "in the amount of" whatever you can pay] if you agree to immediate deletion of this account from any and all credit reporting agencies—Equifax, Experian, and TransUnion. The purpose of this settlement is merely to have this item removed from my credit files. It is not to be construed as an acknowledgment of liability for this debt in any form.

If you agree to the terms and accept this agreement, certified funds for the settlement amount of [amount you offered earlier] will be sent to [collection agency name] in exchange for full deletion of ALL references regarding this account from my credit files and full satisfaction of the debt. As certified funds will be used for payment, there should be no waiting period regarding the deletion of this account from the credit reporting agencies.

Again, my sole objective is to get this item deleted from my file. Once paid, [collection agency name] agrees to delete ALL information regarding this account from the credit reporting agencies WITHIN TEN (10) CALENDAR DAYS following receipt of payment as specified above and will not discuss or acknowledge the debt itself nor terms of this settlement with anyone beyond the original creditor, including credit reporting agencies.

If the above terms work for [collection agency name], please prepare a letter on your company letterhead explicitly agreeing to the same terms as the above settlement offer and have it signed by an authorized representative of the company. It will be implied that this letter shall constitute a legally binding contract, enforceable under the laws of my state.

Your response must be postmarked no later than fifteen (15) days from your receipt of this settlement offer or this offer will be withdrawn and I will request full validation of this alleged debt as provided for by the Fair Debt Collection Practices Act.

Please address all correspondence regarding this account to:
[Your name]
[Your address]
[City], [State], [zip]
[Your email address]

Thank you,
[Your name]

Assuming the collections agency takes your deal, and there's a very good chance they will, you will need to run another credit report to make sure the item is not showing up a few weeks after they agree. If you still see the negative item on your report, you would go back to Step 2 and write to the reporting agency saying that you dispute the validity of the account going to collections. Since, by taking the deal, the collection agency can't talk about your debt with credit reporting agencies, the credit reporting agency legally has to take it off your report.

After you get the collections debt paid off and the collections reporting removed, you may still have to write to the credit card company (as outlined earlier in Step 3) asking them to remove the 30, 60, 90, and 120 days of non-payments before the debt was sent to collections, using any of the templates provided. You need to get the collections ding removed as well as the history of not paying the debt on time. The "not paying" is one black mark on your credit, and debt actually going to a collections agency is a second black mark. If you've done everything correctly, both of those black marks will come off your credit score.

Let's be clear: I am not advocating for lying or blatant dishonesty. The purpose of this section is to help you think through bad credit item removal the exact same way a lawyer or bad credit removal service would so that you can save some money by doing the work yourself. Just as these folks would use the law (as well as polite requests for goodwill gestures) to get your credit back into more favorable standing, so will you.

If you have made it this far, reading-wise, give yourself a pat on the back. Go make yourself a cup of coffee—your mind is probably a bit fried at the thought of all the work that lies ahead. Try to remember a good time in life where you didn't have these problems, and remind yourself that you are on the road back to that place now. Think about shopping for your house.

Back with your coffee? We have a little more work to do.

A high credit score has to do with the lack of bad items on it as well as a certain amount of positive behavior. Remember, good credit is not built by simply having debt but by having a history or record of acquiring and then *paying* debt.

Follow these last tips to raise a "fair" credit score into the "good" range:

- Pay credit card balances and car payments off early and in full (if possible).
- Try not to apply for new credit *unless* you don't have any credit cards. Without any demonstration that you can responsibly take on and pay off debt, your credit score has nothing to go on, so you should get one or two that you can put a few small things on each month and pay off in full.
- Pay utility and home bills on time.

- Put bills on autopay if you are confident you'll have enough of a bank balance each month that none will bounce. If you don't have the confidence of having enough money to pay, set up payment reminders as a minimum.
- Don't close unused or recently-paid-off credit cards. If you have a history of bad credit card debt, it is easy to just close the book and end the nightmare by making the card itself go away. This will only reduce your credit further! Keep it open and put the card in a drawer (or safe) if necessary.
- Set up payment reminders if you think this will help you remember.
- Try to use only 10–30 percent of your credit card limit each month (presuming that amount is something you can pay off each billing period) and pay the entire amount off by the due date, if you can.
- Reduce outstanding credit card balances. Interest on these babies is even worse than your student loans.
- Use a free credit check website to look up your credit periodically. Remember that checking your own credit is considered a "soft" inquiry, which does not affect your credit score. A loan, credit card, or mortgage company checking an actual credit application is a "hard" inquiry, and if you have a lot of these, they will negatively affect your credit score. Sometimes on credit card or refinancing websites, you can run a rate check, where you will see the sentence *Checking your rate will not hurt your credit score.* This means the site is running a soft inquiry.

Above all, try to be patient and practice self-love. If your student loans are in the six figures, *any* amount of interest reduction is going to take literal years off your payback period. To reduce your interest, you need to refinance. To refinance, you need great credit. It's all interconnected. There will be times throughout this process where you feel angry, frustrated, depressed, and just plain bad. You will beat yourself up mentally for getting into such a financial state that these long and arduous processes are required to fix it. Think about steering a giant ship: at times it will feel like you are killing yourself to push the wheel around hundreds of times in order for the nose to move two inches to the left. However, in doing so, you may be avoiding an iceberg!

Notes

1. Erb, K. P. (2018, June 26). What you should know about taxes and student loan repayment. *Forbes*. www.forbes.com/sites/kellyphillipserb/2018/06/26/what-you-should-know-about-taxes-and-student-loan-repayment/#505c47994c88.

2. Consumers Advocate. (Updated 2018, November 28). 10 best student loan refinance of 2019. Retrieved September 15, 2018, from www.consumersadvocate.org/student-loan-refinance/best-student-loan-refinance#list.

3. Tsosie, C. (Updated 2019, August 2). Best balance transfer and 0% APR credit cards of 2018. NerdWallet. Retrieved August 3, 2019, from www.nerdwallet.com/best/credit-cards/low-interest.

4. The best debt consolidation loans. (Updated 2018, September 28). Reviews.com. Retrieved September 18, 2018, from www.reviews.com/debt-consolidation-loans/.

CHAPTER 7

SIDE HUSTLES WORTH YOUR TIME

find the idea of having to work more than one job a major downer, but let's face it: some months we are short on cash, and that's OK—as long as there's a plan for dealing with the shortage. Or maybe you simply want to bank a few extra bucks for a month to put toward your comfort and/or debt.

There are *so* many alleged ways to "easily" earn extra money (both online and in real life), but how do you sort the gimmicky, unreliable, or underpaid ideas from the hustles worth your time? Many of these so-called "jobs" pay under $10/hr, exchange something of actual value for very little money, or subject you to the pain of feeling like you've given up your free time for chump change.

I've compiled a list of extra-income-earning opportunities that I have personally tested. It took me way longer than I expected because so many of the websites and apps describing "easy" ways to make extra money are, in reality, only applicable to people who don't really need much money or are willing to spend a lot of time on a very small payout.

One thing I don't touch on much in this chapter is multilevel marketing (MLM). If you're unfamiliar with the concept, it's where a company uses independent sales consultants to distribute their product. Well-known MLMs are Rodan & Fields, LuLaRoe, Pampered Chef, Avon, Herbalife, and many more. While there are certainly people who find this a lucrative side business, it's something that requires payment upfront for a starter kit or products (which can be costly) and aggressive marketing, which weren't really what I was after here. If you like sales and you're interested in learning more, there are plenty of articles online outlining the pros and cons of joining one of these companies.

My conclusion is that most (if not all) of the "easy," "work from home," and "part time/extra income" opportunities are not worth your time. I will walk you through my experiences and thought process of what to try, what to avoid, and what to warn your loved ones against.

Part 1: Jobs You Should NOT Consider

Please save yourself the frustration, tears, and anger by steering clear of these "easy" opportunities to "make extra income."

Filling out online surveys for money

The advent of the internet has allowed companies of all sizes a wealth of resources to conduct free or low-cost market research online. Research corporations use the average person to take surveys to help their clients gain information, and they offer cash or other reward incentives to volunteers. Popular sites include Branded Surveys (surveys.gobranded.com/take-surveys-online), Pinecone Research (www.pineconeresearch.com), Tellwut (www.tellwut.com), Univox (www.univoxcommunity.com), and many others.

I started trying to list the different sites offering this as a "quick and easy" way to make money and even signed up for a few. There are tons! Unfortunately, from what I can tell, most seem like a waste of time. Many promise to pay you a few dollars immediately just for signing up, but you can't withdraw any money until you reach a certain amount (like $10 or $20), which never happened for me. The surveys are promised to be "fast" but in reality end up taking thirty to forty-five minutes, making the $1 payout anything but worthwhile. About 50 percent of the time, the page times out or you get an error message and have to start over when you get to the end. There are better ways forward.

Driving for a ridesharing service

These are private car-for-hire services that run off an app on your smartphone, like Uber and Lyft.

Maybe you like driving. Maybe you like drunk people. Maybe you like cleaning puke out of your car and watching your insurance premium go up. If not, you may want to consider other alternatives.

There are a lot of internet articles and Reddit threads about these kinds of driving jobs. The people who make the most money, perhaps $400/week, work between 10 p.m. and 3:30 a.m. on Fridays and Saturdays and two weekday nights per week. Uber only covers your car insurance in certain states, and after taxes, the pay breaks down to about $9.50/hour—less than minimum wage in California. This does not count the mileage and depreciation on your car or the pain of trying to rouse a passed-out drunk from the backseat.

"But what about making my own hours? The ease and convenience of hanging out in my car listening to music?" I hear you. If I was sixteen, this would be a cool gig. But I'm not. And neither are you. We are both worth more than $9.50/hour. Do you want to give up your rest and weekends only to find out at the end of an all-night shift you are taking home less than fifty bucks?

Online matchmaking coach

Sites like Personal Dating Assistants (or "PDA": http://personaldatin-gassistants.com/jobs) and Tawkify (tawkify.com/apply/index.php) allow you to set people up on dates or work at home as a "dating assistant." Matchmaking Institute helps interested parties obtain "certification" for matchmaking and start their own online business.

I signed up for two online matchmaking sites to become a paid match-maker. One advertised $14/hr for work-from-home employment. I submitted a lengthy application (complete with essay questions that had to be answered) and was contacted over a month later with instructions to complete an additional unpaid "assignment" that involved making a male profile on a dating website and trying to get girls' phone numbers to "make sure" I could write well. The other company presented a commission-based pay structure that compensated the matchmaker only for dates that actually happen.

In general, I am not a fan of anyone who expects a person to do free work to prove him or herself worthy of the job. With no clear and reliable path toward actually earning money, I'd generally steer clear of these opportunities.

Reviewing jury cases

Lawyers "test drive" cases by using regular people to represent a jury. You can read cases, give your thoughts, and make money through sites like www.jurymatters.com, www.onlineverdict.com, and www.ejury.com.

When I heard there were websites where lawyers "test drove" their cases to regular people representative of their jury, I thought, *Cool!* I am obsessed with true crime documentaries and podcasts, so I'd be totally down to read over some cases and type out my thoughts. Sites promised to pay $25–$50 to read a case and submit my thoughts in "45 minutes or less."

I completed registration at JuryMatters, OnlineVerdict, and eJury. No one ever got back to me. Perhaps I did not fit the profile of what they were looking for. If this sounds interesting to you, I'd definitely recommend making a profile and seeing if you can find paid work—just don't count on anything.

Secret shopping

Also known as "mystery shopping," this is a tool used by market research companies, by watchdog organizations, or by companies themselves to gather info about products. Examples are Bestmark (http://www.best-mark.com/become_a_shopper.htm) and Sinclair Customer Metrics (www.sinclaircustomermetrics.com).

Unfortunately, these were also a waste of time for me. I hate saying that because, again, the whole purpose of this chapter was initially to help readers find reliable sources of side-hustle income. Instead, it became a chapter about how most ideas never panned out. Of course, I acknowledge there are probably some exceptions, and perhaps some of the people reading this book have actually had good experiences with secret shopping.

I personally signed up for Bestmark and Sinclair Customer Metrics to test them out. For the month I was a member, the following "opportunities" came up:

- Seemingly easy things that, when I clicked on the alert email, had already become unavailable.
- Jobs that I could not do because I didn't meet the qualifications. For example: pretending to purchase video games that were more for 15- to 17-year-old boys; dropping off a Buick to be serviced and reporting on how it went—but I don't own a Buick.

In the entire month, I made three dollars for filling out a request for more information on a website and reporting on how long it took for someone to contact me. This almost made me forget the deluge of pointless emails I had been spammed with three times per day. However, between reading the instructions, completing the survey, and taking screenshots, I spent around twenty minutes doing the work, meaning the hourly rate was around $9/hr. This is not a way out of large amounts of debt or toward a house down payment.

Online transcription

Online transcription is the conversion of audio and video files to written documents. Sources of this work include verbalink.com, www.rev.com, www.transcribeme.com, and www.accutranglobal.com.

If you are a writer like me, and a lightning-fast typist, transcription sounds like the perfect job—particularly due to its flexibility and the nonexistence of associated costs such as wardrobe or fuel/commuting. I tried Rev and TranscribeMe. AccuTran Global looked good but was not seeking people who could work the hours I was available. The Rev platform is the most comprehensive, but I didn't pass the online test. I spent an hour doing three minutes of audio, checked and rechecked my work, and found no errors, but still I didn't pass. I'm not sure why.

Here's the problem: transcription is really hard. Jobs claim to pay $20/audio hour, but it took me an hour to successfully transcribe about nine minutes of audio the first time I tried. If you want to know what it's like, try watching a TV show and typing every single word the characters are saying. You must start a new line every time there is a new speaker and follow other formatting rules or you won't be paid. With a lot of practice, perhaps it could eventually become a reliable source of income, but even with my ridiculously fast typing skills, that day didn't look like it was coming any time soon for me.

Search engine testing; "web research"

In this work, you use provided keywords to research the accuracy and relevancy of search results on engines like Google. Based on feedback, the search engine makes changes in the search algorithm.

Search engine testing is another great "make money online" myth. Promises of "easy signup," $10–$20 per ten-minute test, and so forth were present on pretty much every single one of these sites. More annoyingly, many bloggers suggest these sites as sources of extra income for their readers. This is particularly sad, because I feel it provides a false hope for people in financial straits. Hopefully this brief recap of my experience will save you a few hours of time, and you can put that time toward activities that actually make money.

Lionbridge (www.thesmartcrowd.com/workers/job-opportunities)

I spent about fifteen minutes creating an account and application online. I received an email about a week later saying there was a technical problem with my application and that I needed to click on a link and resubmit. The link didn't work. Lather, rinse, repeat.

UserTesting (www.usertesting.com)

I signed up and got a link to take a sample test, but the link didn't work. I updated my Adobe Flash and checked my privacy settings . . . still nothing.

Enroll (enrollapp.com)

Signup took about one minute; the sample test worked, but I then got a message that no paid tests were available.

StartUpLift (startuplift.com)

I registered online and received no email confirmation. I have no idea if anything happened.

Userfeel (www.userfeel.com) and TestingTime (www.testingtime.com/en)

I registered online and received a message that they would get back to me when work was available.

WhatUsersDo (www.whatusersdo.com)

After registration, I had to download their screen-recording software, which I did. I successfully took a five-minute practice test, and it uploaded to the site. I then had to complete a lengthy profile questionnaire. After everything, I was told I would hear a response on the status of my application in one to two weeks. I heard back within ten days and was directed to click a link for availabilities, but by the time

I did, the job was no longer available. With another opportunity, I was supposed to navigate a website and speak out loud and record what I was seeing, but first I was required to take an online survey, and when they asked if I was married and I said, "No," I was told I don't fit the criteria. I think this is a legitimate site and service, but it just feels like a lot of work for so little—or, rather, for nothing.

Appen—formerly Leapforce (connect.appen.com/qrp/public/home) and RaterLabs (raterlabs.appen.com/qrp/public/jobs/list)

I created an online account and registered (you actually need to attach a résumé to complete registration). After several weeks of my application being "reviewed," I heard nothing back but was invited to "continue to monitor" their website for "additional opportunities."

After creating accounts on all of these sites, I did not have the energy to additionally sign up for Validately (validately.com), IntelliZoom (www.userzoom.com/intellizoom/be-an-intellizoom-panel-member/), uTest (www.utest.com), or Userlytics (www.userlytics.com/tester-signup). I had wasted two hours that afternoon and not made any money.

Amazon Mechanical Turk (www.mturk.com/worker)

This is a crowdsourcing internet marketplace enabling individuals and businesses to coordinate the use of human intelligence to perform tasks that computers are currently unable to do.

This one goes down in history for me for being the most extravagant and amazing waste of time. After creating an account, you have the option of completing multiple, hour-long surveys for three dollars, identifying objects in photos—for example, clicking on all of the photos that have trees—at a half-cent a pop, or completing studies that last up to eighteen months and end up paying a total of $9.40.

The one caveat to this is that Mechanical Turk actually does appear to have decent audio transcription jobs, but only if you are already an experienced transcriber. If not, you probably will not pass the test.

Plasma/egg/sperm donation

Plasma donation: plasma is separated from the red blood cells, which are then returned to the body.

Egg donation: a woman undergoes a procedure to extract eggs to enable another woman to conceive or for biomedical research.

Sperm donation: a man provides sperm for inseminating a woman who is not his partner.

Another urban legend of moneymaking! Egg and sperm donation are arduous processes—and if you're not attractive and smart (and in most cases, unfortunately, white), nobody is going to pay for your DNA in any sort of timely fashion.

Plasma donation is a mixed bag. If you live in a large, urban city, it usually involves hours of waiting in rooms packed with people from all walks of life (possibly with different ideas on what constitutes personal hygiene). You can read a book and listen to music to pretend you are somewhere else, but reality will eventually sink in the longer you wait. I think this relative ease or discomfort of this option largely depends on the type of city you're in and the population per capita. If done with some planning and consistency, the payoff can be significant (up to $300/month if you go twice a week), but whether or not it will be a tolerable experience worth your time largely depends on where you live. It may be worth investigating, but it won't make sense for everyone.

Part 2: Jobs You SHOULD Consider (If You're Willing to Invest in New Skills)

Learn web development for free

The Odin Project (www.theodinproject.com) is an amazing resource for people to learn Ruby on Rails, HTML5, CSS3, JavaScript, and jQuery for free. The goal is to provide a complete path for people to go from zero knowledge to employable web developers while working with other students online along the way. The main website is a fully open-source project licensed by MIT. It will take approximately 1,000 hours to learn the necessary skills to actually make decent money either full time at an in-person job or part time or online using Upwork (www.upwork.com), We Work Remotely (weworkremotely.com), Fiverr (www.fiverr.com), or a variety of other sites.

Become a certified Braille (nfb.org/braille-transcribing) or Nemeth Code (nfb.org/math-transcribing) transcriber

Nemeth Code is basically "math Braille." It pays about $3/page for transcribing; a typical high school calculus book can pay $6K–$18K, and you don't need to understand calculus to transcribe. It takes about six months to finish the US Library of Congress Braille class to become a certified transcriber, and it's free to learn. The best part is you can transcribe for the rest of your life when you need cash.

Become a certified dental hygienist, makeup artist, esthetician, yoga instructor, drug and alcohol counselor, life coach, massage therapist, emergency medical dispatcher . . . you get the picture

This path won't be for everyone, as there will inevitably be some upfront costs involved for classes, but if you want to be able to pick up side gigs that don't feel demeaning and/or underpaid that you might actually enjoy, this might be a good route to go. Make sure to investigate local schools, online courses, apprenticeships, and community colleges for the lowest cost. Many offer scholarships.

Part 3: Jobs That Require Pre-Existing Skills

Sell some kind of clever, artsy gadget that you make on Etsy (www.etsy.com)

I actually shop on Etsy a lot. It's a great resource for gift ideas in particular. I am not a crafty person, but if I was, I feel like Etsy would be a great platform. Look around the Etsy site. They post articles on which items have the greatest sales. Jewelry always seems to top the list, as do beads. Handmade greeting cards, on the other hand, are often very low with few sales.

Tutoring/test prep/lessons

All of these actually pay decent money. Tutors for wealthy families can easily make $50–$100/hour. If you got high-ish scores on the SATs or ACTs, you can usually make $25–$50/hr through Kaplan (kaplan.com/work-with-us/join-our-team), Achieve Test Prep (www.achievetestprep.com/careers), or a similar platform. According to Payscale.com, the average hourly rate for a private music teacher ranges from $37 to $62. Easily find opportunities online on Craigslist (www.craigslist.org), Indeed (www.indeed.com), TakeLessons (take-lessons.com/teachers), or post your services on community bulletin boards, grocery stores, and the like.

Online teaching/curriculum author

If you have a master's in something (which is highly likely if you're reading this book), you can probably become an online/remote teacher. HigherEdJobs (www.higheredjobs.com) is the Holy Grail for finding these opportunities (make sure to select "Online/Remote" in the search bar), but other good websites include Indeed (www.indeed.com), SimplyHired (www.simplyhired.com), Google (www.google.com; search "online teaching jobs"), or FlexJobs (www.flexjobs.com).

Translation or subtitling from home

If you're bilingual, there are some companies who offer freelance, work-from-home subtitling jobs, such as Aberdeen (www.abercap.com/careers), Captionmax (www.captionmax.com/workwithus/), VITAC (www.vitac.com/careers/), Rev (www.rev.com), or ZOO Digital (www.zoodigital.com/work-with-zoo/translators/). You can look for additional opportunities on Indeed (www.indeed.com), Fiverr (www.fiverr.com), or Flexjobs (www.flexjobs.com).

Part 4: Jobs That Do Not Require Preexisting Skills

Work a virtual job at a known company

Appen, Apple, Amazon, Humana, Dell, American Express, and other companies actually offer part-time (and even full-time) work-from-home jobs. They can be found here:

- appen.com/careers
- www.apple.com/jobs/us/aha.html
- www.amazon.jobs/location/virtual-locations
- humana.wd5.myworkdayjobs.com/Humana_External_Career_Site (choose the various "Work at Home" options from the left-hand menu under "Locations")
- jobs.dell.com/category/remote-jobs/375/56067/1
- jobs.americanexpress.com/virtual

Apple will require you to have some basic IT knowledge and attend a short (free) training course. I checked these sites at various times and days throughout the month, and not all of them have open applications. Appen actually has the biggest variety and walks the reader through a legitimate cover letter/application process. If you are lucky enough to get one of these jobs, you could feasibly make $10–$20/hour.

Customer service phone jobs (from home)

Visit www.weworkremotely.com for real opportunities to pick up paid customer service or programming work online. Keep in mind that these jobs are legit, so many get a lot of responses. But again, if you are lucky enough to get one, it is a legitimate job.

Become an eBay flipper

Personally, I love old furniture. I love auctions. I like the hunt of finding cool things. Where I live in Los Angeles, swanky-cool furniture by known designers is kind of a hot commodity. When I see a good deal on eBay or at an online auction, I bid the lowest possible price then sell it for more on Chairish (www.chairish.com), Letgo (us.letgo.com/en), Craigslist (www.craigslist.org/), OfferUp (offerup.com), or a local vintage furniture store (which is personally my favorite, because I can just drop it off, take the cash, and drive away). In order to make this work, you need to focus on products you're interested in and know a fair amount about, and you'll also need to understand what those products sell for in your area so that you can be sure to make some money. On Reddit (www.reddit.com/r/Flipping), you can find a lot of people who have made a killing doing this with old video games, car parts, old audio equipment, antiques, and so forth.

Babysitting

That's right—the job you did at age thirteen to make extra bucks for the mall is still one of the best sources of income for extra work. Thanks to phone apps and the internet, it is even easier to find reliable work quickly. Here's a quick lowdown on the best resources:

- **Care.com:** Has the most job options by far, but premium members get priority on job applications. Cost for a premium membership is $37 per month or $147 per year.
- **UrbanSitter (www.urbansitter.com/signup/sitter) and Sittercity (www.sittercity.com):** Both free to find jobs (parents have to pay to use).
- **Sitter.com (sitter.com/babysitter-jobs), SeekingSitters**

(www.seekingsitters.com/becomeasitter), eNannySource (www.enannysource.com/), Babysitters4hire.com: Other alternatives if you want to maximize your chances of finding work.

Prefer to drive kids around instead of hanging out with them? Use HopSkipDrive (www.hopskipdrive.com) or Zūm (ridezum.com) to find jobs where you drive a carpool instead. Both services are kind of like Uber for kids (but are currently only available in a few cities).

Part 5: App-Based Non-Work That Pays

Thanks to technology, there are now lots of apps that allow you to earn extra money "easily." I test-drove some of these options and will share my experience below.

Sell your parking spot

Apps like JustPark (www.justpark.com/about/rent-your-space/), SpotHero (spothero.com/rent-my-parking-space/), and Pavemint (www.pavemint.com/host/) allow you to sell your parking space. I actually signed up for all three and only got one hit in the span of six months, but that might have been due to the hours my spot is available and/or my location. They could be a great resource if you live in a place with high foot traffic and have a driveway so you can leave the availability option on all the time.

Sell your accommodation

In my personal experience, Airbnb (www.airbnb.com/host/homes) is one of the best sources for extra money. I have never operated an Airbnb business (where you never actually live in the property but use it solely as an Airbnb rental), which is verboten in many cities now, but I do use it to back-fill my house with a few guests any time I am traveling or out of town. Depending on what state you live in and your home or condo rules, you may be able to rent to people as a one-off but not operate a full-fledged Airbnb business. You simply clean your house, take a few photos, and list the days you are out of town. It *is* annoying to have to super-clean your place before leaving for a trip and change the sheets when you get home, but if you stand to fund your vacation completely from these small inconveniences, I'd still say it is worthwhile—especially when you consider the alternatives of $11-per-hour part-time jobs.

If you can't deal with the hassle of Airbnb, there are companies willing to take this on for you. Companies like Guesty (www.guesty.com), Pillow (www.pillow.com), and Air Concierge (www.airconcierge. net) can handle a variety of issues like photos, bookings, cleanings, key handover, turnover, and the like. You will sacrifice some of your income for these bookings but free up valuable time.

Pet sitting/walking

Sign up on Rover (www.rover.com/become-a-sitter/), Wag! (wag-walking.com/dog-walker), Care.com (www.care.com), or Barkly Pets (barklypets.com/dog-walking-jobs/) to try and find jobs as a dog walker or sitter. Some are location specific, so check which offer jobs in your area. I have never worked as a walker, but I use Rover all the time to have people let my dog out when I work late. I recommend the service to friends constantly for its convenience.

Rent your car

Phone apps like Turo (turo.com/list-your-car), HyreCar (www. hyrecar.com), and Getaround (www.getaround.com/list) are all apps for renting out your car to strangers. It's kind of like Airbnb for cars. This was difficult for me to test as I live in Los Angeles and am always using my car, but I suppose this could be worthwhile in a place like New York, San Francisco, Chicago, or any other city where a lesser percent of the population owns cars but sometimes needs a car for errands or moving and car owners have access to public transportation to use when they are renting out their car. It could also be an option for people who travel often.

In summary, earning extra money is just as easy or difficult as earning primary income. Don't do it if you can live somewhat comfortably off your primary income; your time and your sanity are more important than a few extra bucks. However, if you can find something to do that you actually *enjoy* and that doesn't make you feel angry, frustrated, or worthless, get out there and do it.

CHAPTER 8

ADDRESSING ISSUES THAT KEEP YOU BROKE

H ave you ever felt a disconnect between what you feel your life is supposed to be and what it actually is? Does the feeling persist year after year, despite you making changes, working harder, refocusing your goals, paying for therapy, getting a significant other, or losing a significant other (lather-rinse-repeat)—and all the while you just keep struggling financially? This challenge persisted through my childhood, teenage years, and early adulthood, and I could never figure out what was going wrong. In short, I had low financial self-esteem—in addition to a laundry list of other problems.

Trauma is generally classified as "an emotional state of discomfort and stress resulting from memories of an extraordinary, catastrophic experience which shattered the survivor's sense of invulnerability to harm."[1] Shortly after the global economic crisis in 2008, Dr. Mark

Goulston identified a checklist for something he called "financial PTSD." Do you suffer from any of the following symptoms?

- Anger and irritability
- Guilt, shame, or self-blame
- Substance abuse, depression, and/or hopelessness
- Suicidal thoughts and feelings
- Feeling alienated and alone, detached from others, and/or emotionally numb
- Feelings of mistrust and betrayal
- Loss of interest in activities and life in general
- Sense of a limited future (you don't expect to live a normal life span, get married, have a career)[2]

When I started to research financial trauma, I realized it was something I had probably suffered from throughout life. And like so many other psychological issues, it is thought to start in childhood.[3]

Maybe your parents spoiled you. Maybe they struggled as children and chose to overspend on you or live beyond their means. As a result, you feel entitled to a luxurious lifestyle—the only problem is that you can't actually afford it. Maybe your family was divided by a divorce. Your parents married, acquired a bunch of assets together, and couldn't afford to keep them when the relationship broke down, so they racked up debt. Maybe they even divorced as a direct result of financial difficulties. Perhaps, even, your parents simply never taught you about money. Our parents' and grandparents' generations thought talking about money was taboo. Therefore, they often weren't so educated themselves or didn't prioritize helping you learn about saving, investing, or debt.

I had the frugal parents. When I was a kid, my parents struggled financially for as long as I can remember. My mother was an elementary school teacher turned stay-at-home mom for my younger brother and me. My father decided to change careers a few years after I was born. For a while, we lived on my grandparents' farm in rural Minnesota. Nobody we knew really had much money, but electricity usage, grocery spending, and bills led to anxiety and conflict almost daily. My parents were too proud (or ashamed?) to ask for help—or receive help, for that matter—and any attempts by family and friends to pick up a bill or pass us some cash were adamantly refused. While they did an amazing job of keeping things afloat, they were unable to hide from my brother and me that a lack of money definitely presented barriers to having fun, looking and feeling good, and developing our interests.

Whether conscious or unconscious, the thought occurred to me that having more money would help me to shed this past and rise above the people whom I perceived as "looking down on me" growing up. I remember wanting to have money so that I could attend whatever school I wanted, buy whatever I wanted, live wherever I wanted, and treat people to dinner and gifts. Whatever happened, I was not going to live like my parents.

As I entered college (a private college in San Francisco, which I paid for with three jobs and a scholarship), my shame and embarrassment about the way I grew up metastasized into a slow-burning contempt—for what or whom, I couldn't exactly say. Life suddenly seemed very unfair. I had gotten a moderate academic scholarship and was suddenly surrounded by "rich" kids. I had thought I could get anywhere in life through hard work and brains, but I started to feel that it was not completely true: kids who came from money *definitely* seemed to have a leg up. They did not have to hold three jobs to pay for their housing and books. They went to parties and on dates instead of working on Friday and Saturday nights. They did not come home from their jobs at 10 p.m. and have to study until 2 a.m. right before an 8 a.m. exam. I felt I had to work a lot harder just to *be* in their world. They never seemed to worry about whether or not there was enough money in their bank account for their debit card to work at the bookstore or whether they had worked enough hours in the month to afford the next tuition payment. They *enjoyed* the college experience.

My contempt morphed into self-pity. *Poor me.* Everyone else's life seemed easy, and mine was hard. Where was my leg up? Why did nothing ever seem to work out? Why did I always seem to work so hard yet could never pay my bills? Why did it seem so hard to ask for better hours, a raise, or a promotion with every single boss I had?

Depression, loneliness, and self-loathing became the general theme of my early twenties. And then I discovered alcohol and drugs.

Drugs and alcohol took the edge off a very painful life. By age twenty-four, I was using alcohol and cocaine almost daily. I did not want to be that person, but I also didn't want to face nor feel severe emotional pain every waking moment of the day. I could not find any other way to get away from the ache. I couldn't even figure out *why* I felt it. The actual factors of my life did not seem that bad—I had not been abused as a child, nobody had died, my parents were still married. I took notice of other people who seemed to have gone through much harder things than me and handled them a lot better. What was my problem? How come nobody liked me or ever wanted to help me get ahead? Why couldn't I get ahead by myself? Did some people get a secret manual for life I had missed? For whatever reason, alcohol and drugs made me hate the world a little less, made me hate myself a lot less, and made work a little more fun. I became addicted to the relief they provided.

Not wanting to admit (or not being able to identify) my true problems of depression, anxiety, and addiction, I convinced myself that the problem was *my life*: where I lived and where I worked, primarily. I needed to find something else to do, some degree to get, where the world would see how special and talented I was and give me the money and respect I deserved. That's when I started taking some classes at San Francisco's City College to discover a new path: filmmaking, with the end goal being New York University's Tisch School of the Arts.

That would show everyone! I thought. I would cease to be a drunk, a party girl, a boring-day-job holder earning $40K/year. Instead, I'd be a master's degree holder and filmmaker. Who knows what would happen next? It would have to be something better than the current state of my life. But how would I get into one of the most prestigious film programs in the country on half a community college class and no prior experience with filmmaking, screenwriting, or a camera? I bought a book on screenwriting and completed the application. I borrowed a camera from a friend and took some photos of another friend. I almost decided not to apply when, just before hitting "submit" on the online submission form, I was prompted to pay an application fee of $140. Clearly, that was throwing away money when it was obvious I had no chance of getting accepted to a program that supposedly got over a thousand applicants for thirty-six grad student openings per year . . . right?

Surprisingly, I did get in. My ego inflated to such an extent I barely saw my own signature at the bottom of the $65,000 student loans at 8.5 percent interest that I signed for the first year of the three- to five-year master's program. I definitely was too excited to read the fine print of the loans, which said that the interest would start racking up each month that I attended school and would roll into the balance upon graduation. What did any of *that* matter? I was going!

I am not saying I didn't genuinely want to study film. While I certainly *did* want to learn and perfect the crafts of screenwriting, directing, and producing, I also wanted to reinvent myself. I thought attending graduate school would magically motivate me to stop using alcohol and drugs. I wanted to feel my life had a purpose, and I wanted this degree to validate me. For whatever reason, I lacked both the self-esteem and the tools to validate myself.

It is important for me to be completely honest in why I *really* went to graduate school and what I was hoping to achieve because it was not just about the degree. I suspect this could be relevant for you too. If we can never be part of the problem—our financial low-self-esteem problem—we can never be part of the solution either. So ask yourself, *really* ask yourself: What allowed you to look past the cost of your very expensive education and rack up hundreds of thousands of dollars of student loan debt? Why was this point so easy to bypass? It was an extremely painful question for me to answer, and only now that I have some time and space between the person I was then and the person I am now can I be honest about my own reasons.

The first semester of film school was great, and my plan to get away and reinvent myself really seemed to work. I had greatly reduced my alcohol consumption, had stopped using drugs, was incredibly excited by what I was learning, and felt I had truly come into my own. It was a happy time. The more class ramped up, however, the more it turned into a pressure cooker. My thirty-five classmates and I, it seemed, were desperate to impress the professors (some of whom were famous directors themselves). The anxiety around making what was deemed a "good" film or writing a "good" script was overwhelming. We went to class from 9 a.m. to 9 p.m. and had to shoot projects for a minimum of twenty-four hours every weekend. Alcohol started creeping back into my life to ease the anxiety. I felt like a fraud. The reality of how much money I was spending started to set in. If I didn't make something of this experience and failed to produce work worthy of Hollywood's attention, it would be a colossal mistake—a failure of epic proportions.

With this conviction and the stress that came along with it, I proceeded to drink my way through a $280,000 education. My degree took five years to complete. I also showed up drunk for most film shoots and one of my unpaid internships. Eventually, I was fired.

Consider how pathetic it is to be fired from an *unpaid internship*. It's basically like saying your contributions actually make things worse than if you weren't there at all. Naturally, I, internalized this to mean my contributions as a *human being* were less than zero.

The most ironic part was that throughout my time at NYU, the vast majority of the faculty told me I was talented all the time. My films were well received. My screenplays were chosen to represent the class on more than one occasion when guest faculty came to town. Yet no amount of praise made me feel good. No amount of success drowned out the *real* problems of my fear, anxiety, depression, and alcoholism. I figured there must be some magic thing I could find that would snap me out of it. If I just found the thing and did it, life would be OK. But I never did.

To this day, I believe that there is no possible way I would be even remotely close to paying off my debt had I not dealt with these issues. When you already feel like your worth as a human being is zero, how can you possibly answer questions at a job interview about salary? How can you ask for a promotion or raise? For me, it was never possible. And when I thought a bit harder about it, I realized that even *before* I started drinking or went to graduate school, a small part of me always felt guilty for just collecting a paycheck—at *any* job. I felt so unworthy of success and money that I convinced myself I didn't want it.

Are you like this? Perhaps you've been both victim and perpetrator. You've let people take advantage of your gifts, and you've also lowballed people who have given you the opportunity. Do you find yourself getting angry when people offer simple solutions to your seemingly complex problems, even taking the side of the people who make it difficult to make ends meet? Perhaps you say things like:

- "Nobody in this field is making money."
- "You don't understand how [my organization/this industry/ the business owner] works."
- "Everybody has to [intern/start at the bottom/survive on very little money] at first."

I told myself these things because it was the only way I could make sense of my hard work never seeming to pay off. It had to be the boss, the company, the industry. It couldn't possibly be *me*.

Let's revisit the idea that if you're not the problem, you can't be the solution either. How depressing is that? For a time, I convinced myself that $280,000 of student loan debt was something that had "just happened" to me. It was the result of a poor system, the school, my bad decisions. Fine. But what could I possibly do about it? Nothing. I might as well just kill myself. People do kill themselves over debt. Cryn Johannsen, founder and executive director of All Education Matters, Inc. (a nonprofit organization dedicated to the eradication of student loan debt), created a blog post titled "Suicide Among Student Debtors—Who's Thought About It?"[4] and asked:

- Have you contemplated suicide because of the amount of student loan debt you owe?
- Have you started engaging in risky behavior (heavy drinking, using drugs, etc.) because of your student loan debt?
- Are you taking medications, such as anti-anxiety pills or anti-depressants, to cope with being an indentured educated citizen?

Here are some of the anonymous responses that appear in the comments section:

"I've started drinking a lot more regularly, especially since realizing that I'll have to go back to get a master's degree to get out of law. Yes, I've considered suicide."

"I don't think I engage in more risky behaviors, but I'd like to."

"Yes, I thought about suicide a lot over the past few years. I take anti-depressants and I had been smoking cigarettes for months, but I did end up quitting. The big issue with that is I want to be an opera singer, so it was my way of giving up. I'm trying to do what I can to get through this and praying for an answer."

"I think about suicide every day. I cannot take it anymore. I get degrading calls all day long from Sallie Mae and Chase telling me how irresponsible I am. All I have done is try to better myself by receiving a college education. I was the first one in my family to go to college and graduate. I truly believed college would prepare me for a successful career and I would be able to pay my loans back. I am making the same amount as I did in college and see no way out. I zero out my bank account each month to pay bills. I don't have anything extra to put toward my loans. All I ever wanted out of life was a decent job, to own a house, and have a family. My credit is ruined, so I will never own my own home. I can't afford to take care of myself, so why would I bring another person into this world when they are set up for failure? If I could afford the liquor, I would drink every night, and hopefully I wouldn't wake up."

"I fully intend to kill myself the moment I finish my PhD, which will be in 8–9 months. I was lucky enough to receive full funding for my doctoral program but carry a great deal of debt from undergrad. I realize now that a PhD in humanities guarantees me a life of miserable poverty and debt-related harassment. That combined with the scorn I know I will face from more successful family members makes life unappealing. I would do it now, but for some reason I'm still invested in finishing my thesis. Not long to wait, in any case."

"Sadly, I can't afford medication or therapy for the anxiety my student debt is causing. I had health insurance through my job for about 9 months before demoting myself (I actually make more money now with tips), and even when I had the health insurance, it didn't cover what I actually needed, nor would I be able to afford copays. So no, medication is not a luxury I can afford right now, and it's directly BECAUSE of my student debt. Funny, I guess, but I'm not laughing."

"I have definitely contemplated suicide. I have $130,000 of debt for a grad degree (not law) that I'm afraid I won't be able to finish, and I honestly can't see any way out from under it. What makes it particularly painful is that I desperately wanted to go to medical school and do some good in the world but am in far too much debt to ever get there now, it looks like (and btw, this particular degree was NOT worth the cost). :(I don't smoke, and if I could afford to drink, I would do it much, much more. No drugs yet (legal or otherwise)."

"I tell everyone I meet that unless they want to never be able to afford their own house, to feed their family, or to have any financial peace of mind, they should run screaming from any form of student loan–financed education. Wish someone had told me that. :("

I don't judge any of these people. I assume that they, like me, did not have white-collar, finance-savvy professionals as parents. I was taught from an early age that education was a good idea, hard work would pay off, and we should always just be happy for what we have. Unfortunately, this advice does not really compute in a world where education costs hundreds of thousands of dollars (often only available through predatory loans), the job market and economy are unstable, and a higher degree may come with a literal lifetime of debt.

That said, there are much better ways to cope with a six-figure student loan bill than suicide. I also don't believe being in six-figure debt requires one to live a life without goals, happiness, or comfort—mainly because I have found a way to live quite well while in debt. Before I learned how to do that, however, I had to do one thing first:

accept that the debt was only a *symptom* of larger psychological and personal issues, some of which require outside help.

For the next few minutes, we're going to look at some of the biggest issues that hold people back. You might find answers and clarity in this section; you might not. Are you ready? If not, ask yourself: Why not? What do you have to lose, besides a bunch of self-defeating attitudes that are holding you back and keeping you in debt?

Depression

I am starting with depression because it's one of those "silent killers." Specifically, it plays in the background of your life, turning everything bad until you convince yourself that there's no hope or point to anything. What a downer. The problem with depression is the same problem that you might find with a lot of the issues up for discussion in the next few pages: most people never think it's "bad enough" to address directly or seek help.

Case in point: I started "feeling down" when I was twelve years old. Many people in my immediate and non-immediate family were medicated for depression, but I had no idea because *no one* talked about it. I spent most of high school in my bedroom listening to sad music. I have college diaries filled with questions like *Will I be alone forever?* and *Am I ever going to stop feeling sad?* I had worked with seven different therapists by the time I was thirty. Each psychologist or therapist had suggested I keep coming for therapy rather than going on medication.

When I finally had health insurance that paid for psychiatric outpatient services in full, I decided to see a psychiatrist.[5] After filling out a series of questionnaires, I was told that I had probably been suffering from depression and anxiety since puberty. I had tried so many different remedies to feel better (working out, changing my diet, drinking, not drinking, getting more sleep, going to therapy, smoking, not smoking, etc.) that I finally decided to try medication.

It was a night-and-day difference. Life was suddenly tolerable—not amazing, but definitely not like living under a raincloud either. I could go to work without tearing up at my desk. I started completing tasks and working toward my longer-term goals. It was amazing. If you think you might be depressed, do not underestimate how much it's affecting your life or how much your life might be improved if you suddenly ditched it.

I've worked with so many people who have gotten on antide-pressants and seen amazing results, especially when combined with counseling or psychotherapy. Unfortunately, every single one—like me—had major hang-ups about getting on meds because we weren't sure if things were "bad enough" to warrant going on medication. In most American states, major depressive disorder is considered a dis-ability. Think about other disabilities: if you were blind, would you just "tough it out"? If you were paralyzed, would you try to handle things on your own—no wheelchair, nothing? Of course not. At the end of the day, there is no harm in seeing a professional and letting them decide whether or not medication could be helpful. What do you have to lose?

Anxiety

Anxiety is another thing that sneaks up on us. When I thought about anxiety as a medical condition, I thought it required curling up in the fetal position on the subway. Nowadays it is often diagnosed with major depressive disorder because the two tend to go hand in hand. If you're always stressed, you're likely to get bummed out about it—and vice versa. Most antidepressant drugs are made to treat anxiety, as well, by limiting the serotonin or dopamine reuptake to your brain, which has an overall effect of feeling less anxious and happier.

If you're not sure whether your anxiety and/or depression are caus-ing challenges in other areas of life, perform an internet search for "online anxiety and depression self-assessment." There are plenty of tests you can take online that, while not as accurate as a professional diagnosis, can give you some indication of whether or not you should seek additional guidance on dealing with either or both things.

Lastly, don't assume that treating your anxiety and/or depression will be unaffordable. Visit your insurance company's website to see if your coverage uses provider networks, which minimizes out-of-pocket costs compared to non-network providers. Make sure you understand your copayments and deductible. In most cases, whomever you are trying to see can have their office look this information up for you.

Addiction and Alcoholism

People in high amounts of debt are prone to abuse alcohol and other addictive substances. In 2012, doctors from the Mayo Clinic found that among 4,354 medical students surveyed, 32.4 percent met diagnostic criteria for alcohol abuse and dependence. Among risk factors showing the strongest association with alcohol abuse were burnout, depression, and low mental and emotional quality of life. Alcohol abuse/dependence was more likely among those who were younger, single, or had student loan debt of more than $100,000.[6] The average medical or law student currently graduates with an average of $159,000 in student debt.[7]

I, too, struggled with alcohol abuse during the height of my student debt balance. I was working several jobs, was living in a horrible apartment, and could afford nothing. Alcohol helped me forget the sad realities of my existence. In fact, it seemed like the antidote to how bad I was feeling, and I didn't care how much it cost to get small relief from that pain. I really hate how society treats smokers, drug addicts, and alcoholics. Addiction is one of the few mental illnesses that has yet to gain acceptance or understanding on a wide scale. Far too many people judge problem drinkers for enjoying the feeling of being drunk, never realizing that it is more about escaping emotional pain than anything else. People in high amounts of debt receive the added bonus of being judged for spending money on alcohol, drugs, and cigarettes.

Do you have a problem with any particular addiction? Only you can honestly answer. The good news is that there is tons of free help all over the world in the form of twelve-step groups, which have helped millions:

- Alcoholics Anonymous: www.aa.org
- Cocaine Anonymous: ca.org

- Nicotine Anonymous: nicotine-anonymous.org
- Overeaters Anonymous (helps with all eating disorders): oa.org/
- Narcotics Anonymous: www.na.org

What's it like going to a twelve-step group? These groups are often misportrayed in film and television. Most of them abide by a common belief that the addiction is a symptom of other underlying problems that must be dealt with to stop the addictive behavior. All offer a free and supportive environment with no obligation whatsoever for visitors to pay or donate money or even return. Members are allowed to choose a "power greater than themselves," which does not necessarily have to take the form of a "god."

Of course, there are many ways to treat addiction, but to my knowledge, twelve-step groups are the most widely available free options. Rehab and therapy can be costly if not covered by insurance. Here is a list of other options that offer affordable addiction help:

Wagner Hills (wagnerhills.com)

Located in British Columbia, Canada. A Christian ministry with a licensed farm facility helping residents deal with different kinds of addictions. Treatment is partially subsidized by the government, and they try to work with every budget.

Second Chance (secondchanceinc.com)

Multiple locations in California. A volunteer-based treatment offering same-day services; outpatient only. Court-issued patients pay a fee; treatment is largely free for other people.

Caron (www.caron.org)

An inpatient program located in Florida and Pennsylvania. It offers zero-interest financing and rehabilitation scholarships.

Siam Rehab (formerly Serenity Rehab; siamrehab.com)

The cost is $6,450 for a 28-day inpatient program in Thailand, and scholarships are offered.

St. Joseph Institute for Addiction (stjosephinstitute.com)

Located in Pennsylvania. It offers scholarships and financing options for a 28-day inpatient program.

Apply for a rehab scholarship with 10,000 Beds (10000beds.org/scholarship/)

Fill out an application online; if chosen, you will receive advice on an inpatient rehab program that is fully funded by donations. Waiting time varies.

See if you qualify for any state subsidy on rehab or addiction treatment

Visit   www.healthcare.gov/lower-costs/qualifying-for-lower-costs/ for more details.

Additional information:

- Rehabs.com: 1-888-341-7785
- American Addiction Centers' 24/7 helpline for free and affordable rehabilitation: 888-523-1524
- Substance Abuse and Mental Health Services Administration (SAMHSA): 1-800-662-HELP (4357)

Personality Disorders

Personality disorders are perhaps the most misunderstood and hardest mental health conditions to diagnose. Many are simply chalked up to the person acting like a jerk. In their most basic form, they are characterized by behavior and thought patterns that are markedly different than those generally accepted as normal for that person's culture.

They are worth mentioning in the context of student loan debt because personality disorders can greatly affect career progression due to perceived or actual difficulty coping in the workplace. For example, they can affect interpersonal relationships with teammates or a boss, impair learning on the job, or lead to substance abuse issues.

In 2005 and again in 2009, psychologists Belinda Board and Katarina Fritzon gave personality tests to high-level British executives and compared their profiles with those of criminal psychiatric patients at Broadmoor Hospital in the UK. They found that three out of eleven personality disorders were actually more common in executives than in the criminals:

1. **Histrionic personality disorder**: including superficial charm, insincerity, egocentricity, and manipulation
2. **Narcissistic personality disorder**: including grandiosity, self-focused lack of empathy for others, exploitation, and independence
3. **Obsessive-compulsive personality disorder**: including perfectionism, excessive devotion to work, rigidity, stubbornness, and dictatorial tendencies[8]

I'm not going to get into the details of each diagnosis here—information is readily available online. Treatment usually occurs in the form of long-term psychotherapy or counseling, and medication is sometimes recommended. You might want to investigate whether or not you have a personality disorder if you:

- have intense but unstable relationships and worry about people abandoning you
- are easily frustrated and have difficulty controlling your anger
- have difficulty controlling your emotions
- blame other people for your problems
- can be aggressive and/or violent
- upset others with your behavior[9]

Attention-Deficit Hyperactivity Disorder (ADHD)

I had a good friend who had worked at the same company for thirteen years, from the time he got out of college into his mid-thirties. After giving much of his life to the company, he watched many of his friends and colleagues get promoted while he stayed at the same position. Upon further investigation with his superiors, he was given some feedback on how he was being perceived in the workplace. Comments like "Doesn't pay attention during team meetings" and "Presentations are too long and all over the place" started to surface.

When he started telling me about the comments, I recalled how my friend was often late to group events (sometimes by several hours, without meaning to be) and how he often started a new conversation in the middle of one we were already having. I asked if he had ever been tested for ADHD or ADD. He hadn't.

ADHD can have huge effects on job search and earning potential. Many times, individuals are perceived as distracted, having poor listening skills, and bad with prioritization and task completion. It can even lead to discord with a team or boss as well as angry outbursts. Friends of mine who were diagnosed as adults had been going through life feeling like underdogs, like they were not as smart as their counterparts, and in complete confusion as to why they could never quite excel at work despite putting in more hours than others.

In addition to struggles at work, managing finances can be a challenge for people with ADHD.[10] CHADD (Children and Adults with ADHD) offers advice on its website for adults with ADHD struggling with finances, such as leaving credit cards at home, making shopping lists, and using a calculator when shopping to add up purchases.[11]

If you consistently struggle with getting organized, procrastination, completing projects, distraction, making careless mistakes, fidgeting, or staying mentally present during long conversations or presentations, you may want to look into the possibility of ADHD being at play.[12] Arming yourself with a full understanding of your shortcomings is the first step toward overcoming them.

Low Self-Esteem

Low self-esteem is perhaps the Mack Daddy of detrimental psychological conditions when it comes to finance. It is a barrier to success of any kind, including—and especially—financial success. Here's why:

It causes you to buy things you can't afford.

Many people with low self-esteem tend to validate themselves through material expressions of success, such as appearance, real estate, cars, etc. In 2010, two social psychologists developed an experiment to better understand why "poor" people tend to spend a proportionally larger amount of their income on status purchases. They concluded that we consume not only to create a façade of success but also to alleviate psychological pain, stating, "Individuals whose self-worth was harmed sought affirmation in high-status goods."[13]

This is one of the reasons I hate traditional debt advice. I suffered from low self-esteem most of my adult life. Even when I was almost three hundred thousand dollars in debt, I spent money I did not have on things like expensive highlights, clothing, makeup, and accessories because my crippling lack of self-esteem told me I *had* to. Thus, the advice of "spend less/save more" was kind of lost on me. It wasn't because I was vain; it was because I was insecure. I did not understand how to reconcile the need to save money with my personal need to gain other people's approval via my external appearance.

It creates short-sightedness.

Confident people make plans, set goals and deadlines, and work toward them. People who lack self-confidence may avoid these things because of an underlying fear or disbelief that they can achieve them. Before working on my self-esteem, I used to look at the bill from Sallie Mae and feel that the situation was permanent. *Someone who got into this kind of debt certainly can't be smart or savvy enough to get out of it*, I thought. I was unable to see a life for myself that involved comfort or financial security. I disqualified myself from any type of help, assuming that my credit was too poor to refinance the student loans, my debt-to-income ratio was too low to get a mortgage, and I could not afford any kind of financial planner who could help penetrate the black cloud of despair. On some level, I probably thought I didn't deserve to be out of debt.

Being convinced your debt is a permanent situation can certainly silence any semblance of a plan to do something about it, thus causing the situation to snowball into more and more debt.

It prevents you from standing up for fair pay and promotion in the workplace.

Anyone who's ever worked in sales can attest to how much harder the job becomes when you don't believe in the thing you're trying to sell. Expecting someone else to determine your self-worth for you will keep you waiting for that promotion indefinitely, will keep you working an unpaid internship well past its due date, and will ultimately make you resent yourself for being seemingly unable to achieve a job you can be proud of.

Most people with low self-esteem are vaguely aware of it yet remain unsure of what to do about it. Self-help books tell us to love ourselves, to open our minds to the wonderful people we are inside, to tell our harshly critical minds to shut up. But it's hard.

There's no formula for fixing low self-esteem, only a laundry list of things to try. Here are some that have worked for me:

1. I tried to stop behaviors that I knew eroded my self-esteem, like smoking and gossiping.
2. I did more "esteemable acts" like calling and texting my friends, saying "Happy birthday" to people on Facebook, smiling at baristas and cleaning people, and offering to help my partner with more around the house.
3. I went out of my way to do things that made me feel good, such as exercising, eating healthy, taking a taxi instead of the train when I was late/stressed/tired, and getting a massage once in a while. These actions helped me tell myself I was worthy of comfort.
4. I started meditation and yoga (albeit sporadically) to try to stay more in the moment.
5. And, yes, I practiced telling myself I was beautiful, cool, pretty, successful enough, and so on when I felt otherwise.

My advice on this one is to stop spending money on books to fix your self-esteem and try to simply *observe* people in your life who seem to have what you want. Take the actions that people with the kind of self-esteem you want take—not the big ones, like marching into the boss's office and demanding a promotion, but the small ones, like being supportive of a coworker—until the actions become natural. If you feel the problem is bigger than this, examine whether you're suffering from depression and seek professional help if necessary.

Affording Help for the Issues Holding You Back

The Affordable Care Act and other policies that came before it (such as the Mental Health Parity and Addiction Equity Act of 2008) have started to categorize mental health and addiction as an essential health benefit. Unfortunately, benefits don't automatically translate into treatment. Copayments and out-of-pocket expenses can still be expensive, even with an in-network provider. Substance abuse treatment centers often have waitlists. Additionally, many psychologists and therapists don't take insurance at all. It is still difficult for the government to enforce mental health requirements. The regulation spans hundreds of pages, which makes it difficult for state health insurance commissioners to regulate all the plans.

The first place to start is your existing health insurance, if you have any. Take the time to read your plan online. Sometimes it covers twelve sessions or part of a psychiatric consultation plus 100 percent of medication. Whatever is covered, take advantage of this first.

After exhausting these options, research free support groups, both in-person ones in your area and those online. Find psychologists in your area and email the ones that interest you, asking if they offer any pro bono work or discounted rates. The more you write about your specific story and situation, the higher the chance they may take an interest in you and choose to relax their normal rates to help. Before I had good health insurance, I got more than one therapist to cut their rates in half, from $120–$150 per hour-long session to $50 per session, solely because I told them the story of my debt.

Contact local university psychology master's degree programs and ask if they offer any discounted rates for sessions with counseling program students who are completing thesis hours. (Almost all master's degree counseling programs require students to complete a certain number of hours of counseling, usually done at extremely discounted rates.) If you ask enough people, my guess is that you will find resources for medication and social support.

The bottom line is: do *not* give up on yourself or the hope of a better life. It is OK to have personal issues that hold you back. Most people have them—and some people, like me, have several! Suffering from addiction, depression, or cripplingly low self-esteem is not your fault. But you can do something about it.

Notes

1. Figley, C. R. (Ed.). (1985, October 1). *Trauma and its wake: The study and treatment of post-traumatic stress disorders.* Psychosocial Stress Series, Vol. 4. New York: Brunner/Mazel.

2. Goulston, M. (2011, August 9). Does the world have financial PTSD? *Psychology Today.* www.psychologytoday.com/us/blog/just-listen/201108/does-the-world-have-financial-ptsd.

3. Hodes, J. B. (2013, December 13). 8 ways your childhood can affect your money habits now. *Forbes.* Retrieved September 14, 2018, from www.forbes.com/sites/dailyworth/2013/12/13/8-ways-your-childhood-can-affect-your-money-habits-now/#68b-4fe8c1ce7.

4. Johannsen, Cryn. (2010, August 17). Suicide among student debtors—Who's thought about it? Retrieved September 13, 2018, from alleducationmatters.blogspot.com/2010/08/suicide-among-student-debtors-whos.html.

5. "A psychiatrist is a physician who specializes in the prevention, diagnosis, and treatment of mental illness. A psychiatrist must receive additional training and serve a supervised residency in his or her specialty. Psychiatrists can prescribe medication, which psychologists cannot do."

   (From www.medicinenet.com/script/main/art.asp?articlekey=5107).

6. Jackson, E R., Shanafelt, T. D., Hasan, O., Satele, D. V., & Dyrbye, L. N. (2016, September). Burnout and alcohol abuse/dependence among U.S. medical students. *Journal of the*

Association of American Medical Colleges, 91(9), 1251–6. journals.lww.com/academicmed-icine/fulltext/2016/09000/Burnout_and_Alcohol_Abuse_Dependence_Among_U_S_.25. aspx.

7. Dancy, K. (2018, May 21). By the numbers: Changes in graduate student debt over time. New America. www.newamerica.org/education-policy/edcentral/ numbers-changes-graduate-student-debt-over-time/.

8. Board, B. J., & Fritzon, K. (2005, March). Disordered personalities at work. *Psychology, Crime & Law 11*(1), 17–32.

9. UK National Health Service. (Updated 2017, Feb 10). Personality disorder. NHS Health A–Z. Retrieved September 13, 2018, from www.nhs.uk/conditions/personality-disorder/.

10. National Resource Center on ADHD. (2017). Managing money and ADHD. Children and Adults with Attention-Deficit/Hyperactivity Disorder (CHADD). Retrieved September 13, 2018, from www.chadd.org/Portals/0/Content/CHADD/NRC/Factsheets/Money-Management.pdf.

11. Ibid.

12. Take an online adult ADHD self-assessment here: psychcentral.com/quizzes/adhd-quiz/.

13. Sivanathan, N., & Pettit, N. C. (2010, May). Protecting the self through consumption: Status goods as affirmational commodities. *Journal of Experimental Social Psychology, 46*(3), 564–70.

CHAPTER 9

METHODS FOR INCREASING SELF-WORTH

I t's 2010. I am working as a nanny for an extremely wealthy family. My hours are supposed to be 9 a.m. to 7 p.m., but I often leave much later. Every day at 6:45 p.m., the kids have a major going-to-bed meltdown that often takes over an hour to resolve. I resent my boss—the mother—horribly. She is nine years older than me and has a net worth in the hundreds of millions thanks to her husband. Most of the time she appears to shop, eat lunch, and gossip with her friends. I am being paid $25/hr in cash every two weeks. The money is often the difference between me eating and not eating that weekend. Unfortunately, the mother often gets busy and forgets which Friday it is, not paying me until Monday. I text-message her reminders, but she doesn't always reply. I spend weekends hungry and crying over the state of my life.

Does this sound like anyone you know? Perpetually overworked, underpaid, and underappreciated? Hating your boss, yourself, and your life? Jealous of everyone doing better than you? The good news: it's all changeable. The bad news: only you can do it.

Self-Respect

I can't tell you how much money I spent on therapists and self-help books trying to learn how to love myself. They all told me to do it, but they never could explain how, and I continued going through life feeling dominated by the elements. I *hated* the topic of self-love and self-respect, had no idea how to make progress in that area of my life, and didn't really believe it would fix any of my *real* problems anyhow. Yet at the same time, I hated going through life feeling like nothing ever worked out and like I picked the losing bet on everything all the time.

Meanwhile, I remained an angry, critical, gossipy, broke, messy person. I cheated, lied, and stole—anything to help even the scales of life and the hand I'd been dealt. I justified my actions, justified hurting people, justified retaliation ten times worse than what had originally been done to me. *If you hurt me once, I hurt you double* was my modus operandi. Friends frequently made their way to my enemy list.

Call it low self-esteem, people-pleasing, or a lack of self-respect. I'm not here to be your therapist, but I would like to examine how all three can have financial implications. We start out with good intentions. We want to be liked. We want to have friends and enjoy a feeling of ease and comfort around others. But constantly being a martyr often causes resentment, which eventually creeps into other areas of our lives.

Do you ever . . .
- say nothing after getting a bad haircut?
- not send your food back if given the wrong order?
- never ask for discounts or negotiate pricing?
- keep damaged groceries or merchandise you paid full price for?
- avoid correcting people who mispronounce your name?

- avoid introducing yourself to a group if your friend forgets to?
- say nothing when you're the butt of a joke or the recipient of a derogatory/racist/sexist/homophobic comment?
- skip personal commitments when asked to work late for no extra payment?
- often find yourself giving people rides or lending money?
- avoid asking people to lower their voices or music when they bother you?
- avoid confrontation when you suspect someone is unhappy with your work or actions?
- attend events out of guilt or obligation (real or perceived)?
- constantly say "Sorry"?
- stay out later than desired if your friends aren't ready to leave?
- say nothing when overcharged for goods or services?
- avoid confronting people who cut you off in line or a conversation?
- feel used or taken advantage of at work or in romantic relationships?
- expect your partner to make you feel better (consciously or unconsciously)?
- remain single when you want to have a partner?
- believe that your parents or another person/place/thing are the cause of your problems?
- believe you are overweight or underweight?
- abuse drugs and/or alcohol?
- ignore your own feelings?
- say statements like they are questions?
- avoid indulging in healthy activities or purchases that would enhance your comfort, safety, or happiness?
- constantly judge others?
- slouch or avoid eye contact?
- base your self-worth on your appearance or other people's feelings about your appearance?
- frequently work jobs unrelated to your goals?
- frequently work for less money than other people in the same role?

I'm not suggesting that engaging in one or two of the above means you definitely have low self-esteem, but if you found yourself nodding your head more than a few times, it might be time to examine the cumulative effect this behavior has on your happiness and well-being.

Sometimes these behaviors fall below the level of our consciousness. Sometimes we justify them, saying "I'm working late because I want to further my career!" or "I don't need to make the rest of my party wait while I have the restaurant cook me a new steak." But almost all of us have known a friend, family member, or coworker who constantly obsesses over what someone else said or did, carrying anger and frustration around for days, often while we sit there wondering, *Why don't they just [break it off/tell the person/do something]?*

A quick Google search on increasing one's own self-love or self-respect usually pulls up cryptic advice such as "Be more mindful" or "Live intentionally." But how do you actually go about this?

Examining the limits of your discomfort

Let's go back to the example about my boss forgetting to pay me on time. I remember having a conversation where friends told me, "Just remind her," or "Just tell her you have to leave by seven." That definitely seemed insane to me. When I was working my fourth unpaid internship, my parents recommended I "ask to be paid for my work." Equally nuts!

If you find yourself constantly feeling like people don't understand your situation or why you can't ask for the things you want in a workplace or relationship, consider that the apparent impossibility might have something to do with *you*. Sure, maybe everyone at your company works late. Sure, maybe nobody in your department makes more money than you. But if everyone in the world thought like this, there would be no billionaires. Some people on your team probably *are* making more money than others; it's time you're one of them. Get comfortable being the exception to the rule.

But what if everything backfires? What if your quest for what you find to be fair and ethical treatment deeply offends the person you're asking, resulting in denial of your request or, worse, termination?

When I was working in a foreign country and my ability to stay in the country was contingent upon my work visa, I had a lot more to lose than a paycheck. If I didn't have that job, I'd have to go home! Combined with my inherent fear of people and confrontation, requests for *anything* in a workplace (even my paycheck on time) felt like a hugely uncomfortable risk.

What convinced me that I had to move forward anyway was a friend pointing out that my current way of working was unsustainable. "Either you get out by 7 p.m. so you can go to yoga and relax or you'll burn out and have to quit anyhow," she said. "Better to take the risk to ask for an on-time paycheck plus a ten-hour workday."

I looked back at past jobs. Hadn't I quit nearly all of them due to burnout, anger, and stress? I had never stayed at any job for more than eighteen months—most were under a year.

Still, the thought of telling this woman "Hey, you need to pay me on time, and starting on Monday, I'm going to walk out the door at 7 p.m. no matter what your kids are doing" filled me with anxiety and fear. What if she simply said "I need someone with a bit more flexibility, sorry" and let me go? How would I be able to get by and stay in the country? My friend suggested that if the conversation felt impossible, perhaps I could write her an email over the weekend instead. This seemed more palatable.

She helped me with the email. I wanted to write my life story, over-explaining how I needed time to decompress so that I wouldn't burn out, overemphasizing how much I loved her family and the job. Too much, my friend said. The end result simply read this way:

Dear _____,

I have a new after-work commitment that will require me to leave your house at 7 p.m. daily. Since the two live-in helpers are always there at that time, I feel confident the kids will be in good hands. Also, this Friday, my pay is due, and the total owed is $_____. My time sheet is on the refrigerator as always.

Thank you again for this opportunity, and I look forward to seeing you Monday.

I almost had an anxiety attack as I hit send. Maybe you are reading this and thinking I'm crazy—who would struggle so much with something like this? If the answer is not you, consider yourself a more highly evolved person than I was at that phase. I had nothing but confidence in the quality of work I delivered, but I always had been very bad at setting healthy boundaries for myself.

I heard nothing back from my boss over the weekend. I went into work Monday, having no idea if she had even received my message. As the clock ticked nearer to 7 p.m., the panic and anxiety started to hit me. *What am I supposed to do—just drop everything and walk out the door?* This may have been doable if it was just me and the live-in staff at the house, but to make matters worse, she was actually home.

The clock struck 6:45 p.m. "Can you take Patrick up to bed?" my boss asked.

Ugh! Patrick was two and seemed particularly amped. I knew it was going to take at least forty minutes to get him down.

Before I could even think twice, the words "No problem" had fallen out of my mouth, and I begrudgingly carried Patrick up to his room to get him into his pajamas, all the while racking my brain to figure out how I was going to explain this completely cowardly behavior to my friend. Once again, I was not communicating my real needs.

To my absolute amazement, however, at 6:52, there was a knock at Patrick's door. My boss appeared. "It's almost seven," she said. "You should go; I'll finish putting him to bed."

I *literally* almost fell out of my chair. She had never offered to help finish a task—ever. She was usually not even home around the kids' bedtime due to outside commitments. As I walked out the front door at 6:55 and got into the taxi taking me to yoga, I felt like I had just pulled off a robbery or something. I could not believe that not only was my email read but it was not even an issue, and I was getting to do what I wanted and what was healthy for me. Though it probably seems like an innocuous story, it was a huge turning point and source of enlightenment to my perpetually terrified, people-pleasing brain. Her reaction went against all of my fears and everything I had assumed it would be. I realized that nobody had been making me a prisoner to these workplace expectations except for me.

If you really can't tell whether you also take too much through the lens of fear and people-pleasing, ask yourself how you react when you see other people having boundaries or asking for what they want. Do you resent your friend who demands her boyfriend get her flowers on Valentine's Day? Do you gossip about the coworker who took extra time off for both Thanksgiving *and* Christmas? If this kind of stuff tends to get under your skin, it might be because you are witnessing people do (and "get away with") things that seem impossible to you.

If having a conversation that will ultimately make you feel better seems impossible, what about a letter or email to that person? What about a journal entry that no one sees? When I was still new to emotional honesty, I did this a lot. I wrote a lot of letters to men that stated my true feelings and then continued to play dating games with them—most of which involved ignoring them and pretending not to be interested at all. Looking at past relationships, I realized that in many of them, I had expected the other person to fix me, make me feel better, or somehow bring happiness into my life. Had I only known that was an inside job.

Acting As If

Andy Warhol is often quoted as saying, "They always say that time changes things, but you actually have to change them yourself." I needed to stop asking for other people's permission to be the person I wanted to be. My entire opinion of my own self-worth was based on other people's reactions to me. They decided whether I was smart, pretty, thin, or successful. Other people's success only heightened my feelings of failure. I had no money, almost $300K of debt, a job I was embarrassed of, and zero love prospects. If "loving myself" or getting a stronger sense of self-worth was the answer, I couldn't find a single self-help book that seemed to provide any practical advice.

The best answer I ever got in response to the question "How do I get more self-esteem?" was "By doing esteem-able acts." *Isn't that what I've been doing all along? I show up for work, don't I?* However, I never really asked people how I could do better—be a better employee or a better friend. I was afraid of appearing too eager in my goals and dreams, so I downplayed pretty much every area of my life, lest actually wanting something or someone exposed me to disappointment and pain.

As I mentioned before, the nannying job led to me working at the hedge fund for my boss's husband. In other words, asking to leave and be paid on time essentially got me a promotion (I think because they respected me more—or perhaps they just couldn't find anyone else). In the elevator of the hedge fund's building one day, I thought about esteemable acts. I recalled how I felt when I was finishing my master's in film and I got to intern for my favorite producer in New York City. It was like a dream. No, I wasn't being paid, and I was pretty much the lowest rung on the totem pole, but I was happy every day I took the train from Harlem to Brooklyn and back to read scripts and make phone calls. It was a memory that contrasted strongly to the way I felt in the elevator and pretty much every day I'd had that job at the hedge fund. I literally *trudged* to work, earbuds blasting angry music until the last possible second before someone spoke to me. I thought that day about a person who might think my job was *their* dream job, like working for a hit television series would be for me.

The elevator doors opened and I stepped out onto my floor, pawing absentmindedly in my purse for my swipe card to get in the office. Like every day for the past two years, I swiped my card and stepped neatly over a messy stack of newspapers that had been dropped off outside the office door—financial publications like *The Wall Street Journal* and *Financial Times*. Every morning, the delivery guys would lean out of the elevator door and throw them at our office, until our office manager (who arrived a little later than me) picked them up and assembled them for reading. My mornings were for getting my boss's trading area set up, and I couldn't be bothered with such menial things that were not my job to begin with.

But how would I act if this was my dream job? Would I have stepped over newspapers that were sitting on the floor at my dream television studio? One day, I knelt down in my skirt-suit and heels and collected all of them. I set them prominently in the lobby for people to read. It took all of three seconds. And then I did it the next day, and the next, and pretty much every day thereafter.

I cannot overstate how this simple act of humility (which I did purely as a sort of acting exercise) revolutionized my life and career. I challenged myself to think of more ways a person who loved my job at the hedge fund would behave. I collected other people's charts off the printer and dropped them at their desk. I said "Good morning" and asked colleagues how they were. I asked my coworker to see a photo of his dog, which I constantly overheard him telling people about. I stopped acting like I was too good to do that stuff (because it was all a cover-up for my low self-esteem anyhow).

Slowly, things began to change. The traders started including me in their daily banter. The office manager and I began taking afternoon coffee breaks. I started getting the office "inside joke" emails and invitations to drinks and dinner. At the start of that job, I had truly believed I was *unworthy* of sitting at a table with people who had millions of dollars and had seen such success in their careers. I assumed I would never have anything in common with them and could never capture their interest, but all of that gradually went away the morning I decided to pick up the newspapers. And over time, I realized that *nobody cared* how much money I had or how successful I was. I was the only one measuring myself by those standards. Tiny "esteemable acts" fixed my low self-esteem.

Year after year, I got raises and bonuses without threatening to quit or even asking for more money. My income doubled and then tripled. I got to do more interesting projects at the office. I started taking little vacations and working out with a personal trainer. I began writing more and entering contests (now that I was not crippled by the idea of rejection)—and even winning some. I hired a writing coach. I opened an investment portfolio. I stopped hating the fact that I had a big chin and extremely pale skin. When I looked in the mirror, I found myself thinking *You're still pretty* instead of the usual *You should get plastic surgery*. When I made mistakes at work or in my relationships, my immediate mental reaction became *Just apologize and move on. Nobody's perfect.* And just like that, I woke up one morning to realize I actually *liked* the person I had become. I still had debt; life wasn't perfect. But I honestly believed I could go anywhere, work anywhere, and talk to anyone—and it was truly amazing. I was no longer a prisoner of my negative, victimized thinking.

So if you've been reading this chapter thinking *Another writer preaching about loving myself and fixing self-esteem—ugh*, stop thinking about the big picture goals and get the hippie woo-ha out of your head. This isn't about singing "Kumbaya." It's about you thinking of the smallest possible thing you can do *today* to start building self-esteem in the background of your life, without therapy, hypnosis, or chanting. Find your one esteemable act. What would a person in your position who loved his or her life do differently than the way you're doing it? It can be as small as just looking people in the eye and smiling. It could be stopping a destructive habit like smoking (for which Chantix is a miracle drug, and often free with decent insurance—but I digress). Pick something, start, then wait.

Invest in Yourself

This is the part of the debt book where I force you to do a budget, eliminate some expenses, and throw a few extra dollars at your student loans every month. Kidding! We put it in a retirement account. Kidding again. We are actually going to free up some money and put it toward *you*, because you're awesome and you deserve to enjoy life and be comfortable.

I'm going to go out on a limb and make an assumption that I wish other debt books had made when I was looking for help. I am going to assume you are *already* a Jedi Ninja of Budgeting. I imagine you know where every single dollar of your paycheck is going before you even get paid, possibly on a spreadsheet. I'm guessing you sometimes use cash to get through tight time periods just to know exactly how much money you're spending. You might eat breakfast and lunch in the breakroom of your office, cut coupons, steal Wi-Fi, celebrate weekend brunch at the sample aisles of Trader Joe's and Whole Foods, and illegally download movies from the internet. Maybe you even do things like rent out your pullout couch on Airbnb, rent out your car and parking space, bike to work, drive Uber, sell your plasma, or pose nude for amateur drawing classes. If you've ever Googled phrases like "can I sell my hair," "learn day trading," or "how to fake own death," don't worry—you are not alone. I have been there—and no, you can't see my browser history.

My point is, the last thing you need is another irritating voice telling you to budget, earn more, save more for retirement, or spend less. I am actually going to tell you to spend *more*—on yourself.

You know how much money you earn and how much you spend. We don't need to go there. Pull up your bank or credit card statement and look for signs of reinvestment. By this, I mean examples of where you used money to *improve* some area of your life. Alcohol and eating out don't count. I am talking about things like going to therapy, getting a massage, taking a class about something you're interested in, attending a seminar, or improving your diet and/or exercise routine. Maybe your building has a crummy onsite gym that you can use for free. We're going to stop using that gym. In fact, we may never go in there again. Instead, we're going to invest in a membership to a nice gym, one with machines that work and personal trainers. Let's stop eating fast food and wearing stained clothing with holes. Figure out where you are cutting corners on yourself.

Challenge yourself to free up a little more money than you thought possible. Perhaps you can carpool to work a few days per week, lower your cable or cell phone plan, cancel a subscription, feed your pet cheaper food, or switch to a cheaper car insurance.

Then think about how to reinvest that money in yourself. A few ideas are:

- **Free:** Go outside, to the library, to an art gallery. Go for a run. Call a friend. Search for outdoor markets or free food festivals in your city. Clean out your closet. Take a nap. (When was the last time you actually took a nap?)

- **$5 extra:** Shop on iTunes. Go to Starbucks. Buy a magazine. Get keys for your house duplicated so you just feel more on top of things. Buy stamps or some nice pens. Go to Fiverr.com—it's an entire website full of people offering services for five bucks.
- **$10 extra:** Take a taxi or Uber somewhere just because. Treat yourself to a movie date. Get the good garbage bags. Go to a car wash.
- **$25 extra:** Go to a concert or community play. Get a manicure or pedicure. Have an organic fruit-and-vegetable box delivered to your door. Have your nicer clothes dry-cleaned. Buy nice conditioner or an "overpriced" candle.
- **$50–100 extra**: Pay someone to come clean your house. Get a massage. Get a Groupon for personal training trials. Visit a nice hair salon that can actually give you a cool cut. Whiten your teeth. Get a new wallet. Buy used designer clothing on eBay. Take someone out on a date.
- **A few hundred dollars extra:** Travel somewhere and Instagram it like crazy. Enroll in music, art, or language lessons. Keep going to the personal trainer. Shop for new clothes. Save for a bigger trip, a new car, or a house. Buy a $200 stainless steel trash bin for your kitchen, or purchase a Dyson to make cleaning more efficient. (You'd be amazed how these kinds of splurges positively affect day-to-day life.)

You get the idea.

When we are strapped for cash, the things I listed above are the type of things that go out the window first. We are taught to feel guilty for simple pleasures and to train our minds never to indulge, scrounging every last penny and putting it toward our debt. And if you enjoy living this way, then by all means, continue. You will probably get out of debt a few months before everyone else. However, when you do, you could also be miserable and resentful.

Reinvent

The idea of reinventing oneself has been implanted in our minds from an early age. We've all seen some form of a movie or TV show when a so-called geek is turned into a beauty and starts attracting new attention—essentially winning at life. I'm not a fan of the mood board or overnight makeovers. When I wanted to kill myself over my financial situation, those were the last things on my mind.

Reinvention or drastic change usually happens as a direct result of some challenge or pain. It is not uncommon for people to "reinvent" themselves every ten years or so, due to a death, a financial crisis, the loss of a relationship, an addiction, an illness, or a desire for career change. You can see many examples of reinvention in celebrities:

- Arnold Schwarzenegger has reinvented himself three times, going from a professional bodybuilder to a Hollywood actor to the governor of California. He did this in the face of a very public divorce (pending the discovery he had fathered a child with his housekeeper).
- Ronald Reagan went from actor to president of the United States.
- Miley Cyrus went from Disney child actor to adult pop superstar.
- Andre Young—more commonly known as Dr. Dre—faced many hurdles throughout his career requiring him to reinvent himself, including the breakup of rap group N.W.A and Death Row Records' legal issues. Through producing and the creation of Beats headphones, he went on to become one of the wealthiest musicians in history.
- Justin Timberlake could have easily ended his pop career after the teen band *NSYNC broke up (who knows what any of the other members are up to these days?). Instead, his career exploded in new directions: a solo music career, acting, and music production.
- Angelina Jolie reinvented herself several times as well, from a sexy action star to a dramatic actress, director, and humanitarian.

It's easy to think of these people and come up with reasons why they did what they did, why they were successful, and why you *can't* be successful. For a second, let's put these doubts to the side.

You are already in the process of reinventing yourself if you take *any* of the suggestions on improving your self-esteem or financial situation. But start by abandoning all labels. You had a successful business or marriage? An up-and-coming whatever? You were the star of your class? A raging addict and manipulator? Nobody cares. Throw these all out the window. Start from zero.

Try to focus on a particular area of your life. Is it finance? Romance? Having direction or a career? Choose one and make a real, physical list of all the things you can think of to help achieve what you're trying to achieve. Here's an example of one I did for this book:

Goal:

Publish a book that helps people get out of extreme student debt and live happier lives.

List of things to do:

1. Figure out how to write a book proposal
2. Research/make spreadsheet of literary management agencies who have proposal submission guidelines on their websites
3. Send out finished proposal to all of them
4. Follow up with emails, calls, meetings with anyone who responds; keep writing book
5. Build website and blog
6. Start doing social networking
7. Do Google/Twitter/Facebook paid advertising if applicable
8. Raise money to hire a PR person
9. Finish book
10. Show literary agent that you have a platform and get them to deliver your book to a publisher

As soon as I finished that list and read it over, the goal felt a tiny bit more achievable. Doing *everything* seemed impossible and overwhelming, but making a spreadsheet did not. It is always surprising how making an action list of items toward a particular goal makes me get it done so much less painfully—not to mention faster.

Please throw out any notion of me doing all these things myself. I took odd jobs to pay for the web designer. I did online fundraising. I hired a writing coach to teach me how to write a good proposal. What I could not do myself, I had someone else do.

However, none of that would have been possible if I hadn't spent time fixing my self-esteem first. I wouldn't have had the confidence to mail out anything, hit anyone up for money, or negotiate lower pricing on services I needed. I had to confront some very personal demons in the forms of depression, anxiety, constant feelings of failure, and active addiction. I can honestly say that none of these things plague me today.

Through honest self-reflection, self-respect, reinvestment, and reinvention, all of us can embark on the process of improving our happiness, finances, and lives. If you focus on your debt or financial situation alone and never address the factors surrounding it, you'll likely be just as unhappy when out of debt as you were in debt. Stop punishing yourself with budgets and unrealistic expectations and allow yourself to think about the life you really want to have—the person you really want to be. It's not an overnight process, but it's also not impossible.

CHAPTER 10

DON'T LET SOCIAL MEDIA RUIN YOUR FINANCES

A ccording to Wikipedia, the American Dream is "a national ethos of the United States, the set of ideals (democracy, rights, liberty, opportunity, and equality) in which freedom includes the opportunity for prosperity and success, as well as an upward social mobility for the family and children, achieved through hard work in a society with few barriers."[1] Nowadays, people have come to associate the American Dream with more concrete ideas around homeownership, education, marriage, health care, and retirement. Many of us feel a societal pressure to achieve such goals or even feel entitled to them.

Throughout this chapter, I'm going to break down where this ideology comes from and why it might be in your best interest to disavow it completely. Whether you are conscious of the pressure to achieve or even consider reaching for the American Dream, I can pretty much guarantee that it's not contributing much to your happiness.

The first version of the American Dream is almost universally agreed to be the US Constitution, and in this sense, it could be argued that the only people eligible to participate in it were white landowners. The essence of the dream had to do with inalienable rights, specifically life, liberty, and the pursuit of happiness.

In the 1920s, the American Dream started being less about rights and more about the acquisition of material goods. The "roaring twenties" are typically thought of as a period of excess, extravagant parties, and Gatsbyesque, larger-than-life characters.

The stock market crash of 1929 put an end to such aspirations. During the Great Depression, Franklin D. Roosevelt spearheaded equal-opportunity homeownership by establishing Fannie Mae to insure mortgages. After World War II, President Truman rolled out the GI Bill for returning veterans, whereby the government paid for a college degree after military service.

Some may say that Truman's "post-war social contract" expanded the Dream to include entitlement.[2] As in, being American meant that people had the "right" to things like education, housing, and health care. But capitalism and a free market economy don't work that way; they guarantee the right to *work* for those things, not necessarily to obtain them.

Ronald Reagan is often thought of as an icon for middle-class conservative thinkers in the United States. The 1950s–1970s were some of America's most prosperous years, where wealth inequality was at its lowest.[3] Thanks to industrialization, manufacturing, steel, and the local auto industry, most families could be supported by Dad's income alone and could afford to buy houses, cars, and home appliances easily.

Let's go back to the American Dream having something to do with social mobility. Social mobility refers to generations of people having more money than their parents or being in a better socioeconomic group than they grew up in. A study from economists at Harvard University and the University of California, Berkeley, examined over forty million tax returns of people born between 1971 and 1993, measuring social mobility. In 1971, a child from the poorest fifth of the population had an 8.4 percent chance of making it into the richest fifth. For a child born in 1986, the odds were 9 percent.[4] In other words, social mobility is not really improving, contrary to the belief held by 52 percent of Americans who think there is "plenty of opportunity" for the Average Joe to get ahead.[5] The study confirms previous findings that America's social mobility is lower than many European countries, such as Denmark, where a poor child has twice as much chance to make it into the top fifth than in America.[6]

Advertising and social media have further morphed the American Dream to be rooted in ideas of happiness acquired through material goods. Over the years, psychologists have tried to understand whether being unhappy fuels materialism, materialism fuels unhappiness, or both. Edward Diener, PhD, reported a narrowing gap between materialists and nonmaterialists in life satisfaction as income rises.[7] Put another way: although the least materialistic people report the most life satisfaction, materialistic people can be almost as happy if they've got the money and means to also pursue soul-satisfying endeavors. The unhappiest people are the ones who have the biggest gap between the material items they want and their actual means to get them.

That said, being materialistic alone isn't always the problem—it's the fact that materialism is often fueled by insecurity. I can personally attest to this. When I worked in the hedge fund industry, we got elaborate gifts for Christmas every year. I never cared about the gifts nor thought of myself as a materialistic person—I had gone to art school, after all. For my first Christmas at the fund, I received a $4,000 handbag as a gift. I remember opening it, seeing this huge beast of a bag. It felt awkward to hold. I questioned whether I should bring it on the subway or leave it at home for special occasions. I was still approximately $200,000 in student loan debt, so I felt sort of fraudulent toting this around town.

However, the bag planted a seed in my brain. It occurred to me that while I was carrying it around, there was no way anyone could tell whether I bought it with my own money or not. I liked the idea of them thinking I had. Next, a tiny part of me started feeling superior to people who did not have an expensive handbag. It was like a Band-Aid had been placed over the shame and insecurity caused by my student loans. I felt a little less shame, and it would have been so easy to confuse this feeling for happiness. But on some level, I knew I wasn't exactly happy either.

Research shows that people in unfortunate situations become more materialistic as they adapt. Teens who reported having higher materialistic attitudes tended to be poorer and to have less nurturing mothers than those with lower materialism scores, a 1995 paper reported.[8] Similarly, a 1997 study headed up by Aric Rindfleisch at the University of Wisconsin–Madison found that young people whose parents were undergoing or had undergone divorce or separation were more prone to developing materialistic values later in life than those from intact homes.[9]

Maybe you're thinking, *I'm not materialistic; I just want to be out of debt.* OK, let's go back to the American Dream. In my opinion, this whole idea of working hard, dreaming big, going to school, following the rules, and reaping the benefits doesn't really hold water anymore. I know a lot of people who worked very hard, dreamed big, went to school, and followed the rules and instead found themselves stripped of monetary gain and beat down by a system that keeps them in crushing student loan debt.

Some of them don't care about owning a nice car or wearing designer clothing. In fact, most don't. But they do want to project the image of a successful life. Just as insecurity drives some people to shop, it drives other people to be more active on social media.

Consider Facebook. We post things, and people react to them. What's going on beneath the surface? A study conducted by Brunel University in London suggests those who are insecure regularly post updates about their relationship status in order to garner attention to distract themselves from their own feelings of insecurity. Conversely, egoists tend to post about their achievements to get likes and comments, which reinforce their sense of self.[10] Thus, social media becomes a petri dish for validating one's personality traits.

Go into your Google browser now. Type in the phrase "Twitter makes me," "Facebook makes me," or "Instagram makes me" and see what Google's autocomplete suggestions for the search are. Almost every response is negative—"anxious," "depressed," "sad," and "jealous" are among the most prevalent suggestions. It's a common phenomenon that has transfixed psychologists for a while. There is no shortage of published research on how using Facebook often negatively correlates with life satisfaction, diminishes self-esteem, and causes anxiety and narcissism.

Before social media, how did we know how other people were doing or what they were up to? Can you even remember? I struggle to. Before the internet, I pretty much only knew about things happening in my family and close friends' lives. There was no army of people from the past to compare myself to. If an acquaintance from high school got married or had a child, I had no idea.

Now, things are different. It is so commonplace for me to meet someone at a professional social event, maybe a friend of a friend, and then add them on Facebook. For the indefinite future, I get reminders of their birthday and see photos of their kids. Or worse—their engagements. There was a time where my social media feeds were so full of engagement photos that I began to think there was seriously something wrong with me because I wasn't engaged. This led to a year of feeling ashamed of myself and my relationship, pressuring my boyfriend (who was not right for me) to get engaged, and generally doubting most of my life choices. Eventually, I turned these viewpoints around, but I wonder whether I'd have felt as down about my relationship had I not been inundated almost daily with engagement announcements from people I barely knew.

There's a term for this: *information overload*. It simply means "exposure to too much information or data." The result is that you either delay making decisions, make wrong decisions, or just feel stressed and overwhelmed.

The combination of insecurity, materialism, and social media can create a repetitive cycle that usually worsens one's financial situation:

1. The debt itself and the financial strain it causes you (possibly combined with the demanding job you force yourself to work) makes you feel stressed and insecure.

2. The insecurity drives you to consciously or unconsciously spend time on Facebook and other social media, looking for approval and/or distraction.
3. While on social media, you can't help but notice other people broadcasting their seemingly better lives, and you feel even more stressed and insecure.
4. Eventually, you go shopping, go out with friends, take a trip you can't afford, and so on, and post about it on social media.
5. You have less money to put toward paying off your debt.

Sound far fetched? Not really. In 2012, a team of Facebook data scientists manipulated the newsfeed pages of 689,003 Facebook users for one week, January 11–18. (If every time you logged in to Facebook that week, your friends seemed to be posting either "15 Photos That Restore Our Faith in Humanity" or more depressing status updates about losing jobs or failing to live up to New Year's resolutions, you might have been part of the study.) The results, somewhat predictably, were that people who saw more positive content posted more positive content and vice versa. Additionally, when scientists removed emotional posts from a person's newsfeed, that person wrote fewer status updates altogether.[11] In layman's terms, it exemplifies that we *do* absorb what we see on social media and it *can* affect us emotionally.

When I was younger, I scoffed at adults who said, "You can't have it all." *Maybe* you *can't*, I thought. Today, however, I believe them— not because I'm jaded, but because I think I am more complex than a job title, achievement, or relationship can define. I can't have it all, because some of the things I want are direct opposites of each other. I wish I didn't have to work, but I want enough money to be comfortable. I think it would be fun to be a working artist, but I need steady income flow. If there is a way to have all of these things simultaneously, I have yet to figure it out. It seems a lot more achievable to learn to be happy with what I do have.

In the early days after grad school, my goals were very small. I mainly wanted to have a job I didn't completely hate. Health insurance would have been nice, but it was not a requirement. A lunch break, hours of operation coinciding with the availability of public transportation—the basics. The thought of buying a house didn't just seem impossible—it was laughable! I literally had *nothing* and $286,000 of student loan debt. My credit score was in the 400s. I lived paycheck to paycheck. Not only did homeownership seem like an idea from another planet, but so did having a wedding, children, comfort, and more! I thought many elements of what I had grown up thinking of as "normal" adulthood experiences were off limits to me as a punishment for taking on too much student loan debt in a creative industry with very little hope for a return on my investment.

It was not completely inaccurate. Without marrying someone a lot wealthier than me, I honestly couldn't afford to throw a huge wedding, buy a house, have three kids, send them all to college, and get home from work in time to cook dinner. I would have to choose one or some of those things; they were not all going to happen.

I'm going to lightly touch on having kids and getting married. I say lightly because this is a very personal topic that includes factors individuals typically consider outside of their financial situations, like what they want in life, what they think will make them happy, and so forth. All I'll say is this: you deserve to have whatever you want out of life. Having student debt doesn't make you any less lovable or any less deserving of success, security, or happiness. Just don't lie to your partner.

Awhile back, there was a *New York Times* article about a man who dumped his bride-to-be not only because she was in six-figure student loan debt but also because she refused to look at or address it.[12] She told her boyfriend she thought she was in about $70,000 of debt, and when she finally looked at her statements when they became engaged, she found out it was double that.

To people without student loan debt, the bride may sound crazy, oblivious, or in denial, but I've been there. My partner taught me how to look at the balance of my student loans without crying. He brought up the topic many times, and we would get into fights for the very same reason as the people in this article—because I simply could not deal with that part of my life without losing it. It was that weighty of an issue. I eventually overcame the fear only after several months of him gently coaxing me to face my fears, as powerful and overwhelming as they were. Remember, I based my self-worth on these numbers—what I looked like, wore, and could buy for myself. Admitting how much debt I had and coming up with a plan to deal with not just the debt but also *my feelings about the debt* was the first step in my financial recovery.

You don't need to put off having a wedding or kids just because you have a low income or a lot of debt. However, you *do* need to look honestly at the debt and choose a long-term strategy that makes sense for your values and true financial situation. You probably can't do everything at the same time.

For example, maybe you and your partner want to get married, and one of you has an ailing parent who may not live much longer. You might prioritize the wedding and decide about having kids or buying a house later. Perhaps you're a woman and you don't have many years left of childbearing age. Obviously, in this scenario, you'd prioritize having children. The bottom line is: all of these things do cost money, and you will need a plan to pay for it. The rest of this book can give you some creative ideas—such as moving abroad, refinancing your student loans, etc.—that can help you set aside the money necessary for the things that will be most fulfilling to you.

It can feel like your student loan debt is a permanent situation, but it's not. Whatever job you're working to pay it off won't last forever. These feelings won't last forever. You won't be broke forever. You don't even have to be broke now. My single piece of advice on the topic of love and kids is simply don't start with the debt; start with yourself. Make a list of what you want out of life and then figure out how those things are achievable *while* you pay off your student loans, not *instead of* paying them—or worse, never experiencing what you want out of life at all. You may need to pick and choose what is happening when. You are worth it, and you are not alone. Happiness is an inside job.

I think we all share the goal of being happy. As in, *really and truly happy.* I would like to focus on two simple and achievable targets for pursuit of this goal, possible at any budget. They are the reduction of materialism and emotional self-reliance.

Reducing Materialism

On a certain level, I've always known that if I could just learn to be less attached to money, possessions, and outcomes, I would be happier. Unfortunately, I have expensive taste—I like to pay people to do things I don't want to do, live in a nice apartment, travel, and enjoy nice things and experiences.

What are the potential fallbacks of being this way? Just ask psychologist David G. Myers, who says, "Compared with their grandparents, today's young adults have grown up with much more affluence, slightly less happiness, and much greater risk of depression and assorted social pathology."[13] Unsurprisingly, ambitious and competitive people are often materialistic. Consumerism is often fueled by insecurity and greed. I think we're all fairly aware of this—and are reminded of it every Black Friday when YouTube videos of people getting in physical fights at Walmarts and department stores flood our newsfeeds.

There's a difference, however, between using money to buy *things* versus *freedoms*. I remember when I spent about $1,500 more per month to live in an apartment where I could walk to work rather than take a forty-five-minute subway ride. For me, it was money well spent. Every day that I did not have to get on the crowded subway made me happy; I came home less stressed and less tired and had more time for myself after work. I felt the increased rent was 100 percent worth the extra expense incurred.

Similarly, I have spent a good portion of money on my own creative projects—writing coaches, website designers, and photographers, to name a few. With other people dealing with the nitty-gritty of my creative goals, I can just focus on making money and being creative. This, to me, works a lot better than working a lower-paying job *and* having to do my own social media *and* make and maintain my own website *and* edit my own photos and videos, and so on. All of that would exhaust me.

The most important thing money can buy is time. Society and the media often associate having money with not having free time. We've all seen TV depictions of the tireless female lawyer coming home late at night only to find the nanny has already put the kids to bed and, thus, having no idea of what else to do with herself, she opens her briefcase and goes back to work at the kitchen table. How many times did the staff of *Mad Men*'s agency sleep in the office? These types of images have built up a negative association with hard work, implying that it is always difficult and all people working long hours are miserable.

Is this really accurate? Let's make a hypothetical comparison. Person A has a 9-to-6 job making $60K/year and working forty-five hours per week; Person B makes $180K/year working over sixty-five hours per week.

Compare their schedules:

Person A (45 hours/week, $60K per year)

6 a.m.: Wake up; take the dog out. Come back; unload the dishwasher; pack a lunch with some of last night's leftovers.

7 a.m.: Start getting ready for work.

8 a.m.: Depart for work. Commute one hour either on public transportation or by car.

9 a.m.–6 p.m.: Work. Use lunch hour to pick up a prescription from the pharmacy and/or dry cleaning.

After work: Rush over to the gym for a 7 p.m. spin class.

8 p.m.: Swing by grocery store.

9 p.m.: Make and eat dinner.

9:45 p.m.: Clean up dinner.

10 p.m.: Take out trash; throw a load of laundry into the washing machine.

10:30 p.m.: Get ready for bed; pack gym bag to take to work the next day.

11 p.m.: Watch TV; sleep.

Person B (65 hours/week, $180K per year)

4:45 a.m.: Wake up; walk downstairs to meet personal trainer at the condo's gym.

5 a.m.: Work out with personal trainer.

5:45 a.m.: Drink a premade protein shake from the fridge; shower.

6:45 a.m.: Drive or walk fifteen minutes to work.

7 a.m.–8 p.m.: Work. Have lunch and dinner delivered to the office (if not in dinner or lunch meetings). Have Skype call with life coach around 2 p.m. to discuss a recent hobby they're thinking of taking up.

8:30 p.m.: Meet a Tinder date or watch game with friends.

10 p.m.: Get home. During the day, the cleaner and/or assistant has done the laundry, picked up the dry cleaning, cleaned the house, and made a protein shake for the following morning.

10:30 p.m.: Sleep.

Is the person working more hours miserable? Is that such a horrible life? I'm not saying one is better than the other—I'm simply saying neither is particularly amazing nor awful. We are complex beings, each with different interests and opinions. I personally cannot stand cooking, taking out the trash, or cleaning my own bathroom. I would much rather put in an extra four hours at the office to have someone do these things for me. Maybe you're the opposite. It's all good.

What the American Dream *should* be today is perhaps an individual right to define and pursue one's personal goals without fear of judgment from friends, social media contacts, or society at large. Rather than simply trying to spend less, we should figure out what we like and dislike spending *money* on and what we like and dislike spending *time* on. Take out a pen and paper and do it now. Here's mine:

> **I enjoy spending money on** people doing my housework, a nice apartment that gives me privacy and a short commute to work, Starbucks, people to coach me to be my best in my goals (both health and otherwise), and travel.

> **I don't enjoy spending money on** electrical appliances and gadgets, a nice car, high-end skincare products, full-price clothing and shoes, restaurants, food, or alcohol.

Notice how I use the word *enjoy*. Yes, you can enjoy spending money! Parting with money doesn't have to feel like doing something terrible or dirty. It can—and should—be fun. Life is too short. The two lists should kind of balance each other out. If they don't, try to make them. You can't like spending money on fine jewelry and not need to spend money on bus fare. Let's be real.

Emotional Self-Reliance

We've talked a lot about being less materialistic and not basing self-worth on appearances. The problem I have with most self-help books is that they talk a lot about *what* to do, and you end up thinking, "Yeah, but *how*?" If you're like me and you spent most of your life feeling bad because you always had less than others, how do you "just" turn that off?

Buddhism often uses the language "freedom from ego" in its philosophy. The word *freedom* indicates a state of not being imprisoned or enslaved, which suggest our egos actually do more harm than good. Below is a list of real things you can try to reduce your own ego and feel better about yourself.

1. Realize that you have a big ego.

Most people do. When I was in counseling for my depression and six-figure student loan debt, my counselor used to call me "an egomaniac with an inferiority complex." It is 100 percent possible to have a big ego and low self-esteem, and for me, it was a pretty terrible combination. But recognizing that you have a big ego is the first step to doing something about it.

2. Try not to take things personally.

If someone doesn't like you, it's their problem. Being yourself means not being affected by outside influences.

3. Stop complaining, and let go of the need to win.

When we attach our self-worth to winning or losing instead of simply performing to the best of our abilities, we set ourselves up to feel bad. It is simply not possible to win 100 percent of the time.

4. Realize you don't always have to be right.

When feeling uncomfortable about being misunderstood or my point of view not being taken seriously, I try to ask myself, *Do you want to be right or do you want to be happy?* We tend to think they go hand in hand, but they don't. I'd rather be happy.

5. Stop defining yourself by your job, your relationship status, or your achievements.

We are so ingrained to answer the phrases "Tell me about yourself" or "What do you do?" by immediately bringing up materialistic indicators of success. This could be a job title ("I'm the creative director of _____" or "I work at a hedge fund") or some external acknowledgement of talent ("I just had an article published in the *New York Times*."). Fight the urge to define yourself this way. When someone asks you what it is you do—even if you *did* just publish an article in the *New York Times*—try to talk about what you do (writing) without the attachment. Attempt to talk about your job without inserting your title, accolades, or a company name.

My first attempt to do this was to practice saying that I was an executive assistant. My ego would always want to insert that I made $165K/year or was only doing that job because it didn't drain me creatively and I could keep up with my writing, but I got used to just saying the words "I'm an executive assistant" or, alternatively, "I am a writer, but I don't do that for a living right now" and realized that people could and would draw their own conclusions no matter what I said. If people wanted to think *Executive assistant—what a broke loser*, I had to accept that. If people wanted to think *A writer who hasn't published anything—must not be good enough*, I had to accept that, too. I have zero control over how other people interpret the external facts about my situation.

What I learned through years of doing this was that when people see that you don't define yourself in such parameters, they have a harder time doing so. It is never your problem if other people don't like you just the way you are.

6. Walk away from big egos inviting you to a conflict.

When someone else's ego challenges yours and you react in a way you're not supposed to (i.e., not rising to the bait), they usually retreat or back down.

7. Remember that another person's reflection of you is a message of who you are.

In the Mayan tradition, there is a greeting called *Lak'ech Ala K'in*, which typically translates to "I am another yourself." It has several meanings; most have to do with how we are all one, how our actions affect others, and so forth. It also means, however, that when we hurt, it's not someone else's fault but our own, and it's possibly an indication that additional inner healing or learning needs to occur.

8. When you realize you have been done wrong, forgive.

Do not retaliate. Do not avenge. Do not manage the situation with your bruised ego.

9. Change your attitude about failure.

Consider how much people avoid going after their goals due to the fear of failure and how much of this fear is based in ego. Try to get clear on what "failure" on a specific goal would actually look and feel like. Remind yourself that what failure looks like on the outside isn't necessarily a failure to the person who allows him/herself to make and learn from mistakes. In other words: other people thinking you failed doesn't mean you actually did.

10. Realize when you're playing the victim.

Sometimes people don't listen to our ideas and our work goes unnoticed. A common and very egocentric reaction that is also self-sabotaging is

There's no use; no one listens to me. By focusing on yourself as a victim as opposed to where you can improve, you may end up giving less than your full potential.

11. Start believing other people have something interesting to say.

It sounds so obvious. However, it's worth pointing out that if you approach situations assuming people don't have anything to say, your ego precedes you. Approach social situations as if you are a documentary filmmaker or a journalist. Challenge yourself to find that one interesting thing. Don't turn the conversation back to you. Don't name-drop.

12. Practice mindfulness or meditation.

C'mon—you knew it was coming. I'm not saying you have to sit on a rock under a tree for thirty minutes per day. Do whatever works for you: a guided meditation podcast, emailing a friend a recap of your day, or just spending a few minutes before bed in silence, reflecting on the past twenty-four hours.

13. Stop looking for faults in others.

The ego loves finding fault in others because if they're not as good, they're not a threat.

14. Force yourself to view "difficult people" differently.

I could write a whole separate book about this. During my years in finance, I came across plenty of angry, abusive people. At first, I slumped into a depression over what I perceived as daily humiliations, usually taking the form of someone screaming at me for something. I experienced the same type of people while working on film sets. I honestly feel like I have spent the better part of my adult life around explosive personalities. Over time, I convinced myself that their outbursts usually didn't have anything to do with me but were a response to everything else going on in their lives. Shifting my outlook made working with them ten times easier, because once I took myself out of the picture, I simply saw flawed people with whom I could practice empathy. Somehow, this felt very freeing.

Ready to hold hands and sing "Kumbaya"? OK, seriously . . . if you're thinking *But I wanted to learn how to pay off my student loans* and are feeling annoyed at me for spending so much time talking about ego, I'm sorry. I only bring these things up because they have made a real difference in my happiness and my ability to work toward my own goals, both financial and otherwise.

Emotional self-reliance can take several other forms, often playing a role in romantic relationships. Looking for our partner (or "a" partner) to make us happy usually backfires. The path to emotional independence usually follows the same steps as reducing ego. It's all connected, and it's all leading to one place: your happiness. I once heard a friend say, "When I stopped trying to make ten dollars, I made a hundred." Maybe it's a famous quote; I'm not sure. I didn't really understand it at the time, and I remember thinking, *So, I should just stop trying to pay off my student loans and they'll pay themselves off? Yeah right!* That seemed so dumb.

But now, I think I do understand what it means. My experience has been that when I stopped attaching myself to the *outcome* of paying off my student loans, I learned how to be happy with the *process* of paying them off and the other stuff happening in the meantime. When I redirected my feelings of shame and failure over my financial situation into renewed energy for the job and relationships in front of me, they got better, I got better, and my debt became easier to pay off. I made more money, and more opportunities came my way.

My advice is this: Forget about the American Dream. Focus on *your* dream and on getting in touch with your highest self—a self that isn't driven by fear, materialism, and ego. See if your financial situation changes as a result, and while you're at it, check how happy you are too.

Notes

1. American Dream. (Updated 2018, December 7). Wikipedia. Retrieved November 12, 2018, from https://en.wikipedia.org/wiki/American_Dream.

2. Amadeo, K. (Updated 2018, October 29). What is the American Dream today? The Balance. Retrieved October 16, 2016, from https://www.thebalance.com/what-is-the-american-dream-today-3306027.

3. Piketty, T., & Saez, E. (2003, February). Income inequality in the United States. *Quarterly Journal of Economics, 118*(1), 1–39. http://piketty.pse.ens.fr/fichiers/public/PikettySaez2003.pdf

4. Mobility, measured. (2014, February 1). *The Economist.* Retrieved October 17, 2016, from http://www.economist.com/news/united-states/21595437-america-no-less-socially-mobile-it-was-generation-ago-mobility-measured.

5. Dugan, A., & Newport, F. (2013, October 25). In US, fewer believe "plenty of opportunity" to get ahead. *Gallup News.* Retrieved October 17, 2016, from http://www.gallup.com/poll/165584/fewer-believe-plenty-opportunity-ahead.aspx; *The Economist*, Mobility, measured.

6. *The Economist*, Mobility, measured.

7. DeAngelis, T. (2004, June). Consumerism and its discontents. *American Psychological Association, 35*(6), 52. Retrieved October 18, 2016, from http://www.apa.org/monitor/jun04/discontents.aspx.

8. Kasser, T., Ryan, R. M., Zax, M., & Sameroff, A. J. (1995). "The relations of maternal and social environments to late adolescents' materialistic and prosocial values." *Developmental Psychology, 31*(6), 907–14.

9. Rindfleisch, A., Burroughs, J. E., & Denton, F. (1997, March). Family structure, materialism, and compulsive consumption. *Journal of Consumer Research, 23*, 312–25. https://www.jstor.org/stable/2489568?seq=1#metadata_info_tab_contents.

10. Connor, L. (2015, May 22). What do your Facebook status updates say about you and your relationship? The results may surprise you. *Mirror.* Retrieved October 19, 2016, from http://www.mirror.co.uk/news/uk-news/what-your-facebook-status-updates-5741866.

11. Hill, K. (Updated 2014, June 29). Facebook manipulated 689,003 users' emotions for science. *Forbes.* Retrieved June 28, 2014, from http://www.forbes.com/sites/kashmirhill/2014/06/28/facebook-manipulated-689003-users-emotions-for-science/#5340f5ff704d.

12. Lieber, R. (2010, September 3). How debt can destroy a budding relationship. *The New York Times.* https://www.nytimes.com/2010/09/04/your-money/04money.html.

13. Myers, D. G. (2000, January). The funds, friends, and faith of happy people. *American Psychologist, 55*(1), 56–67. http://www.davidmyers.org/davidmyers/assets/1_Funds.friends.faith.pdf.

CHAPTER 11

YOU ARE NOT YOUR DEBT

I never wanted to be an addict, suffer from depression requiring medication, or get myself into almost $300,000 of student loan debt. But I also never dreamed that these exact situations would lead me on a journey that helped me improve my relationships, my self-love, and my finances tenfold. It used to annoy me when people said "Everything happens for a reason" until I noticed that I have always emerged from bad situations a humbler, more well-rounded person. Throughout the years, my debt has forced me to rethink all of my choices and realign my ideas of who I am and who I want to be.

As I wrote this book, I connected with many other people who are dealing with high student debt, unhappy careers, and general feelings of hopelessness about their future. I return again and again to the topics of self-esteem and acceptance. It's easy to downplay the very real consequences of debt on the human psyche and spirit. In reality, I have found debt to be almost as traumatic as the death of a loved one. This chapter deals with the *emotions* that come with debt.

Acknowledge that it's a really big deal. It transforms life. It requires a complete healing process—a point that seems to be missing from all of the other debt books I read. It seemed like every place I turned to for help or advice just told me to suck it up and stop going to Starbucks.

What I realized was that going through the process of dealing with my issues, financial situation, and career path very much followed the five stages of grief, from denial to acceptance. How does your situation align with the process of grief? Understanding this path can help put our lives in perspective and help us more quickly through the stages to acceptance—and to becoming as happy as we pretend to be on Facebook and Instagram.

Stage One: Denial

I refused to look up my debt balance for years or accept that my struggles with addiction were negatively affecting every area of life.

After finishing school and consolidating my student debt to automate the minimum monthly payments under an income-based repayment (IBR) plan, I never looked at the balance of my debt nor the progression of paying it off again. I figured the amount was so large it didn't even matter what the actual number was—a hundred thousand dollars and a million dollars felt equally impossible to pay off.

I lived in the fantasy that none of this mattered because under the income-based repayment plan I was on, whatever was not paid off after twenty-five years would be forgiven anyhow. When I explained this to my [not American] boyfriend at the time, he was skeptical.

"Forgiven—are you sure?" he asked. "They just go away completely?"

"*Yes*," I insisted, thinking that is what the US government had promised. I'd read it on a bunch of different websites, several times.

He proceeded to drop the five words that still haunt me to this day: "*But what if they're not?*" He encouraged me to find and read everything I could about this income-based repayment plan, which was a new policy at that time.

I finally decided to read the fine print. It said that the loan *is* "discharged" or "forgiven" after twenty-five years of perfect, on-time payments but that whatever the end amount came to would count as taxable income. With around twenty-two years left and 8.5 percent interest on an already-six-figure balance, I would owe approximately $236,000 in taxes by the time I was in my fifties.

To this day, I still meet people with an IBR plan who think their student loans will be completely forgiven after their twenty-five years of minimum payments, not knowing the remainder will be taxed as income. It still takes some digging to find this information on the IBRinfo.org website.

I had lived in the fantasy of being able to pay the minimums and then have the rest be forgiven completely because it was a lot easier to do that than consider the possibility I needed a plan to pay off almost three hundred grand. I was essentially living in denial.

Similarly, for most of my twenties, I refused to make the connection between the unhappiness I felt around my love life and career and my struggles with drug and alcohol addiction. My attitude of "You'd drink, too, if you had this life" simply dragged out the process of dealing with my problems, adding years of pain and dysfunction to my story while adding to the list of things I said I would never do yet did. If you can relate to this, just realize that no one (including and especially me) is saying your pain isn't real, but it doesn't serve in any useful way and you owe it to yourself to get some help.

Stage Two: Anger

I was angry at my school, my parents, the income-based repayment website, the government, and God.

The whole realization about forgiven student loans becoming taxable income hit me pretty hard. I decided to meet up with one of my grad school teachers that day at Starbucks. I got my soy cappuccino and went over to her.

"How's it going?" she asked.

I proceeded to hysterically break down in a pretty crowded reading area.

A couple of days later, I met up with another friend at Salad Stop.

"How has your week been?" she asked.

Another public meltdown ensued, complete with hysterical crying.

It was hard to stop thinking of myself as a victim. At that time, there was no indication in my life that I would ever earn more than $70,000 per year. I'd live a poor, destitute life in crappy apartments, never traveling, never having anything nice, until I turned fifty and filed for bankruptcy.

I continued to be angry for two more years. After working multiple internships in Los Angeles and New York, I found out that the "jobs" I was hoping to get promoted to paid about $85/day (as a production assistant) or $30K/year (doing development for a production company)—money that was insufficient for even *existing* in cities like LA and New York.

My very first year working as an executive assistant paid about $45K/year. It was extremely painful for me to reflect on how if I had just gone into the film industry immediately after college and worked my way up the ranks, I would probably be further along than having gone to grad school and amassing a ton of debt. In addition, my student debt made it impossible to even work in the film industry while living normally and paying off the loans. I felt like a fool.

I was also pretty angry that the 8.5 percent interest rate on my $286,000 loan was a massive hemorrhage. Here, however, I allowed that anger to move me into action. My sole focus in life became refinancing to a lower rate. I had a giant spreadsheet of all the companies I could find who offered to refinance student loans at a lower rate. SoFi, CommonBond, Earnest—I applied for all of them, several times. The rejections rolled in: my income wasn't high enough, my credit score was too low, the loan amount was over their max limit. I put dates on the calendar of when I would apply again, three to six months after the rejections. Every time I got a bonus or a raise, I'd try again.

It was very easy to see each rejection as another reminder that I was an idiot, a loser, unworthy of their time, help, or money. My anger kept me going. I was enraged at the high interest rates, and even if I got another reminder that I wasn't good enough, I just kept trying.

Stage Three: Bargaining

"I'll work at a job that has nothing to do with my goals or dreams as punishment for my bad choices, but only for a few years."

Working a job I hated from 6:45 a.m. to 7:30 p.m. most days of the year (including public holidays other than Christmas Day and New Year's) was the price I told myself I had to pay as punishment for my poor financial choices. But it would only be "for a few years," I reasoned. The universe must reward such efforts, no? Maybe if I worked a few years doing something I didn't want to do, I'd be out of debt and get back to my dreams.

There were consequences to working in Singapore and being so far away from my roots. Over five years, I missed my grandfather's funeral, the birth of two close cousins' children, and countless weddings, birthday parties, and housewarmings—and I'm still not out of debt! But I paid off over $150,000.

I learned how to get really good about giving the CliffsNotes version of why I lived there. It boiled down to: "Because I am in a lot of debt and I have a good job." And I did. Some days it felt that I had been making payments forever and would never get to the end—I still feel that way sometimes. What gives me greater comfort is choosing to accept and live with my choices. Day by day, it gets easier to choose this route instead of hating myself.

Whatever choice you have to make to get out of debt, own it. Learn to love it. Learn to learn from it. It's possible—I promise. I like and admire my colleagues, and I learn from them daily, in a way I never thought possible in the beginning.

Stage Four: Depression

Depression is a very real thing. Debt is a very real contributing factor.

I remember the day I discovered LoanGifting (www.loangifting.com), the crowdfunding website where you link your student loan accounts and ask family and friends to contribute to the balance. *What a great idea*, I thought, almost unable to click "create an account" fast enough. After creating a profile and plugging all of my information in, I looked at my profile and the numbers underneath it. I was so ashamed at how high the debt was that I could not finish and publicize the account.

I played around with refinancing at different periods of life, trying the five-, seven-, and ten-year payoff plans. Sometimes I would get too ambitious and pick too high of a monthly payment, thinking I'd just scale down my spending and give literally all of my monthly income to those loans, only to have to lengthen the term because I couldn't. I further beat myself up when I had to extend the term again after moving back to the United States and having less disposable income than I'd had abroad. It felt bad, thinking at one point that I was three-and-a-half years away from paying off all the loans and then having that number become seven years. Ultimately, I chose to lengthen the terms so I could simultaneously save money at a higher return rate and buy a house to live in.

Toward the beginning of my debt process, I went on antidepressants because I was just so sad about the state of my life with the debt. (They helped a lot. I highly recommend seeing a psychiatrist if your depression gets so bad you are missing work and barely participating in life.) Depression is a very real thing. Debt and addiction are very real contributing factors. Don't cut yourself off from living, and recognize that it might require some time, money, and professional help to deal with.

Stage Five: Acceptance

As a direct result of dealing with my debt and issues, I started dealing with myself. I began to live.

Today, I can truly say that I have come to a place of acceptance with my career, my financial life, and myself. This is not to say there aren't some days when I backslide into anger or depression (for example, the day one of my classmates from film school was nominated for an Oscar). When I need to refinance my loans to a longer term, or when I fall short of being able to pay my credit card off to the absolute penny one month, I actively refuse to see this as a reflection of my self-worth.

Sometimes I like to think about why these situations came into my life. Before them, I was such an arrogant person. To some extent, I really did think there was something special about me that should allow me to get a free shortcut toward fame and fortune. One time, a woman who was in Alcoholics Anonymous told me that after she had her driver's license taken away for drunk driving, she had to carry around her passport to prove her age at bars. She told herself that it was actually better to carry her passport around, "you know, just in case." She meant, *just in case* fame and fortune hit and she needed it to be whisked off to another country. She was drinking at biker bars in rural Iowa, but in some strange corner of her mind, she actually convinced herself that the night might possibly end with someone taking her on an international flight.

Maybe I was also a bit delusional, investing so much money in such an uncertain career. That arrogance was quickly wiped away when I found myself getting my boss's coffee every morning in Singapore. Once that arrogance (and the fear that was underneath it) went away, so did a lot of other insecurities. I started entering writing contests, going out on more dates, painting my toenails hot pink. As a direct result of dealing with my debt, I started dealing with myself. I began to live.

Ironically, while acceptance is the final step in the stages of grief, it is the first step in most recovery programs. Most people say that only when they accepted themselves as an alcoholic, drug addict, gambling addict, or the like could they start dealing with it. The quickest way out of *any* type of anger, depression, or pain is acceptance. Acceptance means accepting you're human. You make mistakes. You have needs. You're not perfect.

For me, acceptance also means that I have no idea what strange path my life will take. It will, most of the time, not be in the place or with the person or in the exact condition I wanted. Had someone told me that a direct result of taking a babysitting job in Singapore would find me six years later sitting on a private jet in Paris, I would never have believed it. Things have turned out infinitely weirder, crazier, and more hilarious than I ever would have dreamed. Have you ever heard the phrase "You can't write this stuff"? That's a phrase about regular old life.

The more I accept every part of myself, the easier it is to accept other people. The more fully I accept my mistakes, the more quickly I accept other people's less-than-great choices. The less I punish myself, the more I can say, "Yeah, let's go there; I'm trying that." I refuse to make myself a prisoner of my consequences. I refuse to stop living life.

Your story won't be the same as mine. We may not have the same resources, salaries, opportunities, or amount or kind of debt. You might not be the kind of person who writes affirmations on Post-It notes to stick on the mirror or goes to twelve-step meetings. The point is that changing your financial situation (and life) in a meaningful way goes way beyond budgeting and penny-pinching. Canceling your cable subscription or moving back in with your parents while failing to address or examine the actions and attitudes that caused your financial insecurity will only result in a lifelong battle with chronically undervaluing yourself—a problem much worse than your debt.

My vision for you and for myself is that we accept where we're at in life; that we have a job that we kind of like and feel more than fairly compensated for; that people respect us and we respect ourselves; that we are loved; that we live in a place we enjoy with a mortgage we can afford; that our hopes and dreams feel within the realm of possibility; and that we fully experience life. If that reality feels very far away, it's OK. Start by shutting out the voices that say you'll never amount to anything, that you're a loser, or that your financial situation indicates something about your value as a human being. You are priceless, wonderful, and beautiful, and if you need to enjoy avocado toast once in a while to be reminded of that . . . buy it.

ACKNOWLEDGMENTS

I have to start by thanking my former partner, Pete, who encouraged me in my writing every day of our relationship. I know you didn't always understand my need to bolt out of bed every morning, but your support never wavered. Thanks also for giving me the courage to face my financial situation and showing me that people with a ton of student loan debt are still worthy of love (and sometimes even business class!).

Thanks also to my parents, who kept our family afloat with their blood, sweat, and tears and worked miracles daily on the tightest of budgets. I know it wasn't easy. I'm sorry for not being more appreciative. Little brother, I love you unconditionally. May you find peace and happiness.

To my writing coach, Caroline—this book would simply not exist without you. There were many periods when our relationship was the only thing keeping the creative part of me alive, and for that, I am eternally grateful. You have an incredible gift of helping people bridge the gap between self-doubt and their goals. Working with you each year added meaning and purpose to my life in a way nothing else could have.

To Brittany and Adam—I shudder to think what my life would look like had we not met. Adam: you taught me everything I know about tenacity, and I truly feel I can do anything after working for you. Brittany: your generosity and the opportunities you fought for on my behalf changed my life. Why you repeatedly looked out for the underdog Midwestern girl, I'll never understand. You singlehandedly restored my faith in humanity. Thanks.

Thanks to my editor, Katie, for your support and encouragement every step of our process, and to everyone at Familius for making this all happen.

George: I don't understand how we found each other in this crazy world, but every day I am happy and grateful we did. Never change

And finally, to my friends in sobriety—you know who you are. I look forward to continuing to trudge the road of happy destiny together. Thank you for my life.

ABOUT THE AUTHOR

STEPHANIE BOUSLEY grew up outside St. Paul, Minnesota. In 2001, she earned degrees in international business and psychology from the University of San Francisco, but she became increasingly interested in film and music. Upon graduation, she turned down an analyst position at Citibank, opting instead to run music bookings at a nightclub while attending film classes. In 2007, Stephanie decided to focus on filmmaking and apply to graduate school. She was accepted to New York University's Tisch School of the Arts, where she served as Todd Solondz's teaching assistant and earned an MFA in film production.

As part of her thesis completion work, Stephanie produced several of her classmates' films in Singapore, India, Nepal, and the Philippines—living in Singapore during pre-production periods. Stephanie decided to stay in Singapore rather than return to the US. Eventually, after many different jobs—from nannying to tech start-ups—Stephanie ended up working for one of the world's most successful hedge funds and became the assistant to the CEO. Being surrounded by people earning tens of millions per year (instead of carrying six-figure debt) taught Stephanie a whole new way to think about money.

While abroad, Stephanie never stopped writing. Her teleplay, *Savage*, won Script Pipeline's First Look Contest in 2014, as well as Screencraft's Pilot Launch Competition.

Stephanie currently resides in Los Angeles, California, where she lives with her dog, Kaia.

ABOUT FAMILIUS

Visit Our Website: www.familius.com

Familius is a global trade publishing company that publishes books and other content to help families be happy. We believe that the family is the fundamental unit of society and that happy families are the foundation of a happy life. We recognize that every family looks different, and we passionately believe in helping all families find greater joy. To that end, we publish books for children and adults that invite families to live the Familius Nine Habits of Happy Family Life: *love together, play together, learn together, work together, talk together, heal together, read together, eat together,* and *laugh together.* Founded in 2012, Familius is located in Sanger, California.

Connect

- Facebook: www.facebook.com/paterfamilius
- Twitter: @familiustalk, @paterfamilius1
- Pinterest: www.pinterest.com/familius
- Instagram: @familiustalk

The most important work you ever do will be within the walls of your own home.

CPSIA information can be obtained
at www.ICGtesting.com
Printed in the USA
BVHW080124131219
566397BV00008B/15/P

9 781641 702386